Fishing the Maumee River
Walleye Run

by
Brian Miller

Published by
Brian Miller
PO Box 282
Sylvania, OH 43560

Library of Congress Control Number: 2012903171
ISBN: 978-0-615-60392-6

Cover photo by Engbretson Underwater Photography
Photography by Brian Miller
Illustrations by Julie Gottardi
Edited by Jennifer Miller and Kevin Roach

Dedication

This book is dedicated to my dad,
Norb Miller, for sharing time with me regardless
of whether it is fishing the river or working on the
house. Although he does not share the same
passion for the outdoors, his selflessness and
desire to help are inordinate. Sharing those times
with you working at my side has created
wonderful memories.

Table of Contents

Acknowledgments

When I dreamed up the idea of writing a book about fishing the Maumee River Walleye Run so many years ago, it was not about writing a book at all. To me it was about sharing over twenty-five years of experience with others in the fishing community. I have found so much enjoyment in sharing this information, whether it is through the pages of a book, in magazines, or in person. In these past years I have had so many talented fishermen on the river help me become the solid fisherman I am today.

Although I could have sat down and written reams of pages on the Maumee River, not all of this information was dreamed up on my own. There have been so many friends and family members that have contributed their talents to make this possible. My older brother, Jeff Miller, was the first to bring me down to the river to get me hooked. Then through my college years he drove me back and forth every weekend so I could fish the walleye run. My father, Norb Miller has also shared the river with me mostly for the conversation and quality time.

All of those along the way who taught me the river, God knows you each spent endless hours with me. I spent countless hours watching and learning from the best walleye fishermen. All of these people are amazing fishermen. Each of you know who you are, many I have known for over two decades.

Writing and designing a book expands far beyond being a talented fisherman. It took blood and tears to scribble out the workings of this project. Some of those who helped me along the way are talented individuals that kindly offered help when most needed. My sister, Julie Gottardi, who has an astonishing graphic design talent. She worked endlessly to build graphs that have so wonderfully depicted my words. Kevin Roach, a brilliant man, ensured the grammatical mistakes had been wiped clean. Bruce Farrar, with his layout advice and editorial talents to help all the pictures appear perfectly.

Most of all I would like to thank my beautiful wife for allowing me to work for countless hours. Although I am sure she was tired of listening to me ramble about walleye she continued to support my dream. Her soft words and amazing knowledge provided the help I needed. I could not have become an outdoor writer without her editing skills. She is amazing at making sense of the words I etched and swept away many grammatical faults that would have crept onto the pages.

Thank you to all who contributed to my fishing knowledge, graphic design, editing, or sharing the majestic Maumee River.

About the Author

Brian Miller had the great opportunity to grow up near the Maumee River. He was only 10 years old when his older brother, Jeff Miller, first took him down to the river for the experience of his life: the Maumee River Walleye Run. Since then he has not missed an opportunity to fish the entire season.

Growing up he looked up to outdoor writers reading books and magazines from cover to cover. Finally he decided he too wanted to share with others what those legendary outdoorsmen did for him. Miller's passion for the outdoors was sparked and has been burning since. This drive pushed him to become more involved in the outdoors. At last, he found a niche for his talents and became an outdoor writer. Miller's primary focus is writing about his outdoor strategies. Each year he contributes his expertise to many local and national publications, often appearing in Michigan and Ohio outdoor publications.

He has taken the opportunity to share his 25 years of Maumee River fishing knowledge. Over these years there have been many changes in fishing techniques. Because he loves river fishing there is always a drive to become better at catching walleye. This drive has placed Miller on the cutting edge of his strategies trying new fishing techniques each year.

Miller quickly learned that every day and season he spent on the water taught him a new lesson. These lessons are what he enjoys writing about. His words are brimming with wisdom, presented in a lighthearted, entertaining style.

Introduction

At some point, most anglers realize their sport is so much more than catching a walleye. For me, it is the enjoyment of the spring sun warming my face on a cold morning. It's the time shared with my father and brother on the water. It's the cold splash of water from a walleye as I release him back for another day. It's the feeling of excitement when the reel screams out a cry from a walleye.

The exhilaration overtook me at a young age and keeps me traveling back to continue the quest each year. It has been 25 years since I began my journey. Today I feel the need to share those experiences with others standing along the shores of the Maumee River. Inside these pages you will find a lifetime of experience fishing walleye on the river.

The purpose of this book is to help you become more knowledgeable about fishing the walleye run. There are special techniques that only work here, secret tips only known by local fishermen, and timeframes to target trophy walleyes. When I look over the river there are more unproductive locations then productive. In these pages I will walk you through identifying the key locations regardless of the weather or river conditions. This will unlock the key for success even under the toughest conditions of rising water or cold fronts.

Beyond techniques I have had the opportunity to study the walleye senses. A scientific look into walleye has helped me understand why some fishing techniques work and others do not. We will dig deep to explain vision as it relates to lure color; taste and smell as it relates to impregnated and spray on scent; lateral line and hearing as it relates to lure vibrations and boat noise.

The ultimate question is answered within these pages. Where are the best locations to fish for walleye on the Maumee River? This book reaches far beyond the basics techniques, perfect for a novice or experienced walleye hunter. This is the most extensive information written on the Maumee River Walleye Run today. I firmly believe the knowledge and experience you will glean from these pages will help you become an extremely successful walleye river fisherman.

Chapter 1

Yesterday, Today, and Tomorrow

The legendary spring Maumee River Walleye Run is a big deal to local fishermen. As the weather breaks and frozen ice washes down the Maumee River, anglers almost immediately begin trying their luck in the icy water. During the annual run, tens of thousands of walleye swim upstream to spawn while thousands of fishermen come to enjoy the sport. This is the largest run of walleye east of the Mississippi and causes people from dozens of surrounding states to drive in for the event.

The excitement felt about the Walleye Run almost surpasses anything else for the avid fisherman, drawing large numbers of anglers to the river. As a result of this much activity, fishing the Maumee River takes a special technique that is different than other walleye fishing done in the Midwest. The massive amounts of people, cold water, and restrictive regulations make the annual Walleye Run a challenge for many. Once a fisherman has learned some of the advanced fishing techniques this fishing can be quite exciting. I warn you, once you have been bitten by the walleye bug it will be hard to shake. This is an addictive event that will keep you returning for the rush of walleye year after year.

Over the years I have guided many people in the Maumee. This has taught me so much about how others fish and what makes up a great Maumee River fisherman. I will describe those experi-

ences throughout this book so others can achieve the fishing success they crave. To fully understand the impact of fishing the Maumee River we need to look at the makeup of the river, key triggers for the walleye run, and our outlook for tomorrow's fisheries.

THE MAKEUP OF THE MAUMEE RIVER

The "Mighty Maumee" is just that: mighty. It is the largest tributary draining into the Great Lakes. The river basin covers 8,316 square miles that includes 17 Ohio counties, two Michigan counties, and five Indiana counties. Two rivers, the St. Joseph and St. Mary's, merge in Fort Wayne to create the Maumee River. From there it flows for 25 miles through Indiana then another 105 miles in Ohio until it discharges into Lake Erie. The Maumee River drains many different tributaries including the Auglaize River, Beaver Creek, Blanchard River, Swan Creek, Tiffin River, and Tontogany Creek. These are only the main tributaries, and do not include all the drainage from the smaller creeks and ditches.

Along the river are several islands that add to the natural scenery. In the small stretch ranging from Waterville to Maumee are the Indian, Missionary, Granger, Butler, Blue Grass, Audabon and Marengo Islands. The most popular for walleye fisherman is Blue Grass Island. Occasionally locals to the region will refer to the Maumee basin as the Black Swamp because historically the river basin was primarily wetlands called the Black Swamp. In the 1850's, settlers began draining the areas for agricultural use. Today, rich farmland stretches through the Black Swamp territory.

The beauty of the river resonates with anyone visiting the Northern Ohio region. Since 1974 portions the Maumee River have been declared a State Scenic River and a State Recreational River. Along the river are 30 parks to provide public access and preserve that natural splendor. The portion of the river that possesses the best natural spawning gravel runs through the Side Cut Metropark. The scenic park has captivating scenery nestled along the shorelines. A walk down the exquisite trails will almost always guide you toward some wildlife. The whitetails and waterfowl are abundant making this a place to take in a breath of fresh air. Throughout the year many families, runners, photographers, naturalists, anglers and everyone in between share this exquisite Metropark.

With hundreds of walleye being harvested each day the Maumee and Sandusky Rivers still only account for 5-10% of the total walleye harvest each year.

THE WALLEYE RUN

More than 25 years have passed since I started fishing the walleye run. This was an exciting time for me with excesses of time to fish. All that time did not give me the experience I needed to effectively catch limits of walleye. I can admit that I made far more mistakes than anyone should have to agonize through.

Back then there was not much information about fishing technique. I remember like it was yesterday when I received my first hunting and fishing magazine. Immediately I sunk into a chair for hours reading it from cover to cover. Today is a different era; we have more information than ever before. In the last decade there have been countless new techniques and a refinement of lures to help catch more fish. Fishing the Maumee River during the spring walleye run takes special techniques that can rarely be found between the pages of a magazine. Before discussing how to target walleye, it is important to understand the walleye run today.

During the summer months, many of the larger walleye move North and East in Lake Erie. Then during September and October as the fall colors begin peaking many of the walleye begin to migrate back to the Western Basin. This movement makes for some of the most amazing big fish catches. Most winters the river freezes over, then once Mother Nature loosens her grip the ice begins melting and eventually breaks up and washes out of the river. This is an amazing view if ever caught. At this point there are few fishermen who get the urge to fish. There is still a considerable amount of warming that needs to be done before the main spawn, although there are resident walleye that can be targeted year round.

At this time of the year the water temperature is close to freezing and will slowly warm. As the water temperatures rise walleye begin spawning into the Maumee, Sandusky, and Lake Erie spawning grounds. Walleye often spawn around the country between 40 to 52 degrees Fahrenheit, while in the Maumee walleye most often spawn between 42-46 degrees.

The saying goes that Spring Showers bring May Flowers; instead it should say Spring Showers bring March Walleyes. Okay, that doesn't rhyme. Anyway, the melt from the winter's snow and spring showers cause the river to rise, preparing the river for the walleye run.

There are a number of influences which start the spring spawning, some of which include water temperature, river flow, and photoperiod, which is the hours of daylight. Weather plays a large role. Since there are low numbers of walleye present all year long in the Maumee River there are some local fisherman in February and early March who start targeting those fish. Often by mid-March good quantities of walleye are beginning to run into the river system. This timeframe can be feast or famine depending on the weather.

A few years back there was an extended period in mid-March when the mercury rose far above normal levels. For several days there were record highs. Many trees woke up from their winter hibernation. All around there were flowers pushing up from the ground, flowering trees budding, and grass showing new life. We were a month ahead of schedule and the walleye responded. The river temperature skyrocketed and large spawning schools moved up the river. Never before have I seen such a strong spawn this early.

Stepping into April is when most of the spawning schools

push into the river. Several times throughout the season spawning groups of walleye push up the river. The weather in April is far more stable than March. In April, the weather warms throughout the month. Given those facts, I still see a snow fall each April. It does not last long, but occurs most years. The record high for Maumee, Ohio was 89°F in 1942 and the record low was 8°F in 1982. On average it is 48°F (100 year average). As you can see weather can vary greatly during the spring months.

When the female walleyes first arrive their eggs are hard which means they are not ready to spawn. As the proper weather conditions and timing approach they become loose and are ready to spawn. But even when the conditions are right, female walleye do not all spawn at the same time. Different schools (runs) of walleye arrive at different times and those in the river also do not spawn at the exact same period. Once spawned out, females almost immediately return to Lake Erie while the males (jacks) stay for a longer period. Some quickly move back to Lake Erie while others stay for nearly a month. This leaves fish scattered throughout the river during the post-spawn period.

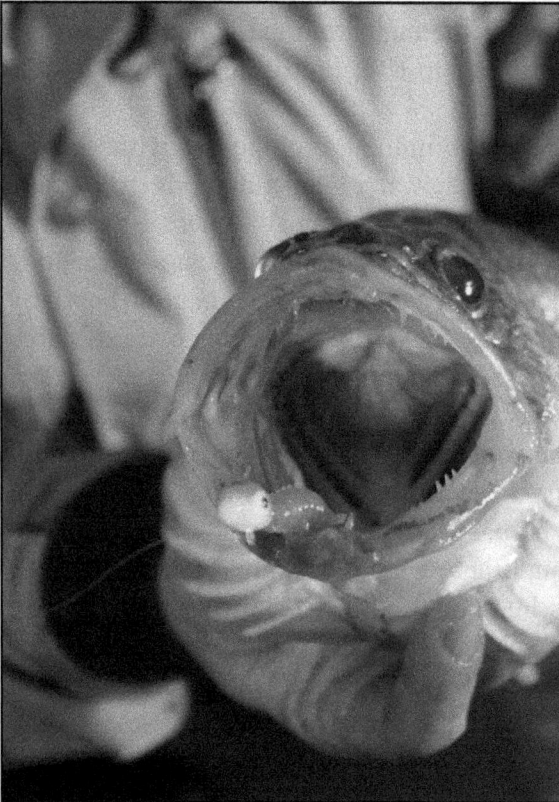

Water temperature is not the only determinig factor of the walleye run. There is also the river flow and photoperiod (hours of daylight) which are equally important.

42 - 46 degrees is the ideal temperature range for spawning conditions but a quick rise in temp. means walleye will spawn in warmer water.

Throughout the month of April there will be many great days to fish. Traditionally walleye will spawn from the last week in March to the second week in April, although I have seen these time frames vary greatly from year to year. As the month of April progresses and the water temperature continues to increase there are also other fish spawning in the river. The Maumee River has a huge population of White Bass that run up the river, with an ideal spawning water temperature around 55 degrees. They arrive at the end of the walleye run when the warmer water temperature is right for their spawning.

So many anglers think the arrival of the White Bass signifies the end of the Walleye Run. This is untrue. The warmer water temperature often means the walleye have spawned but there are still countless opportunities to target post spawn walleyes. This takes a different approach but can be a successful timeframe.

WALLEYE TODAY

Lake Erie in 2012 is holding 22 million walleye two or more years old, with the record high in 1988 when there were 77 million. How many of those walleye typically spawn in the tributaries? Jeff Tyson, ODNR Fish Biologist Supervisor, indicates, "That is the million dollar question. Many have speculated but we do not have that data." This is some of the research they are conducting to understand the fine details on fish movement within the Great Lakes. Anglers in the Maumee and Sandusky Rivers only account for 5-10% of the harvest each year, which is 30-40 thousand walleye.

The walleye population can recover very quickly; one of the latest spawning years (2003) produced 68 million walleye. Tyson has indicated that walleye over 30 inches may date back to good year classes from 17 to 18 years ago. There have also been walleye caught in past years that have been as old as 26 years. It is amazing

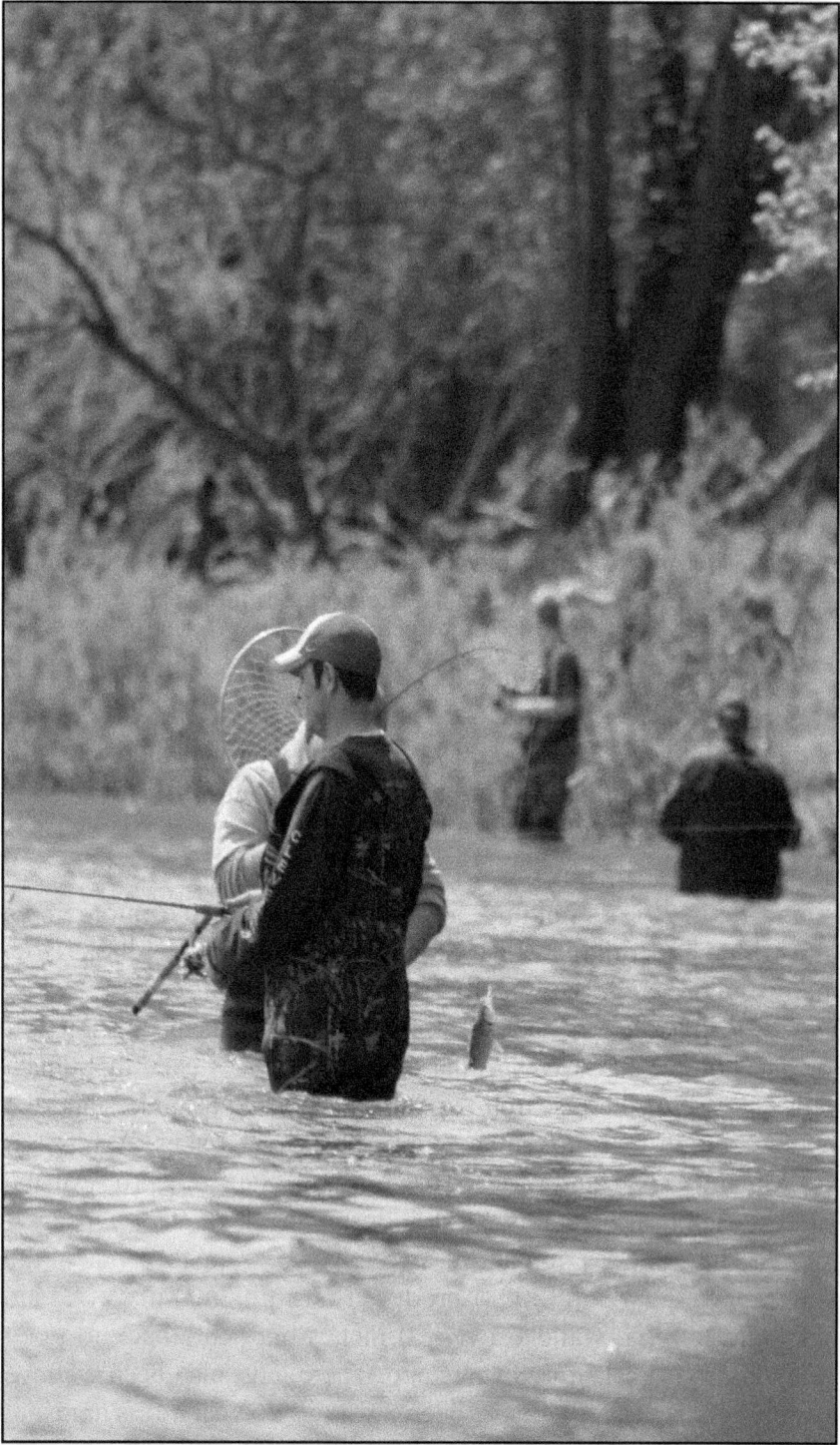

to comprehend that a walleye can be that old.

Years with larger classes of fish produce walleye that grow at a slower rate initially, while some of the smaller classes can produce fish that grow at a faster rate initially, but as they grow older the growth rates balance with all the other classes of walleye. Then some of the smaller classes actually produce faster growing fish initially. It is common to catch walleye in the larger size range of 19 to 28 inches. Along with those there are fish over 30 inches long and weighing 10 lbs caught every year. The spring walleye run is one of the best opportunities to capitalize on a walleye that qualifies for a Fish Ohio pin. A Fish Ohio walleye must measure a minimum of 28 inches. The current Ohio state record is 33 inches long, weighing in at 16.19 lbs from November 1999.

We have a wonderful fishery today and with the work being done by many of the biologists it should continue into the future. Whether your goal is a shore side lunch or a state record walleye the Maumee River has something to offer.

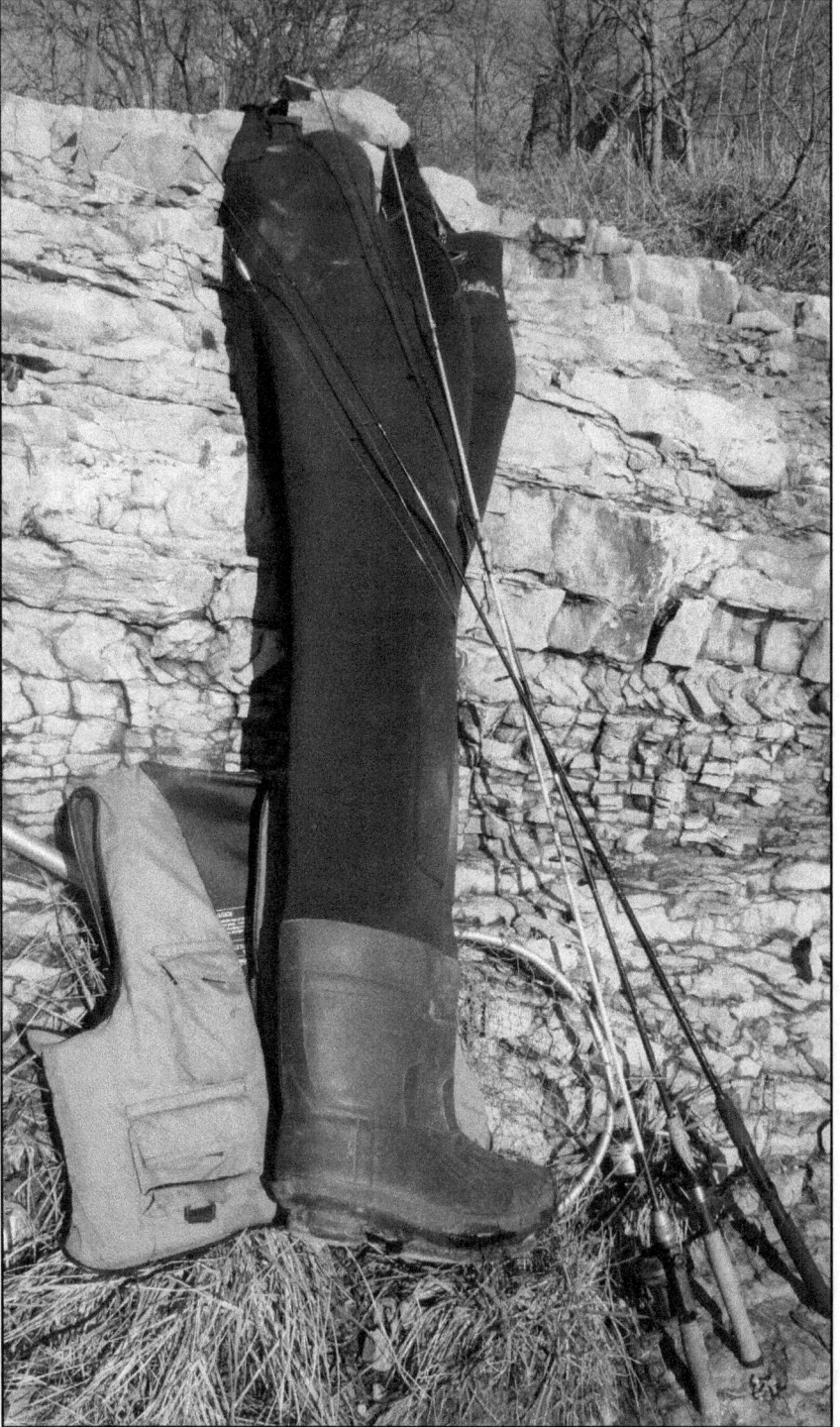

Chapter 2

Equipment Insight

Today walleye fishermen have an array of gear to consider before stepping into the water. It is amazing to see how manufacturers have continued to enhanced equipment each year. In the early 1980's I was fishing in cold, bulky rubber waders but today warm neoprene waders have become the norm.

When considering rods, waders, stringers and everything in-between; there is a predominant difference between high quality tackle built for hardcore fishermen and substandard gear. Furthermore river fishing has its own special attributes, which takes gear that can withstand the tough environment. I have tried some rods that make better whipping sticks and stringers that loose more fish than they hold. On the other hand there are some wonderful products that make fishing more enjoyable. Great gear augments a skilled angler.

RODS

Fishing in a larger river system requires a rod with enough backbone for pulling large walleye while providing the sensitivity for subtle bites. So let's discuss rod sensitivity; what is needed and what is not. The more sensitive rods are developed from graphite. Graphite rods which are built with higher rating of graphite modulus, are lighter, and more sensitive. The high level of modulus also means the rod

Quality rods provide the sensativity to feel every
rock, stick, or fish on the bottom of the river.

can take less abuse. Sensitivity comes with a tradeoff so finding the right balance for you as a fisherman is necessary.

Often rods will be rated by the IM or modulus within the rod. The higher the number the higher the quality of rod produced. A few common standards are IM6, IM7, IM8, etc. Some manufacturers use the IM standards while others rate by the modulus. Unfortunately manufactures do not have a standard for what qualifies in each category. So an IM8 can range from one company to another.

High-modulus graphite is used to increase feel into the fisherman's hands. When looking for a rod I am searching for a rod that provides the most amount of feeling transferred into my hand. Walleye fishing the river is a jigging game and the more feeling transferred through the rod the better opportunity for feeling the bite. A one piece rod is the way to go. They carry feeling through the rod much better which means improved sensitivity. Only when space is a determining factor do I consider trading performance for space with a two piece rod.

Match your gear with the type of fishing you plan on doing. This equates to adding backbone into your river fishing rod. I like a challenge therefore overpowering a walleye is no fun for me. Adding the right amount of backbone allows the fisherman to fight the current, the walleye, and successfully stay clear of other fisherman.

On many occasions a medium action rod is the best option. It provides the strength to pull in a large walleye while dealing with the toughest currents. As the waters drop below normal river levels and the season grinds on a medium-light action rod is a better choice. Under these lower water conditions the medium-light action allows a finesse technique that brings on more fish.

In tune with sensitivity comes the action and sensitivity of your rod tip. Feeling each rock the sinker hits and when a finicky walleye bites on your lure makes all the difference. For these occasions walleye fisherman prefer a fast action tip. This allows an

High-modulus graphite rods do not always come with a high price tag. Know what to look for to capitalized on some great deals.

angler to cast jigs easily while feeling the lightest tap. Line guides are another consideration; look for aluminum oxide or better guides. These types of guides will handle all lines including the tougher braided line.

It is only after spending countless days on the river that an angler learns to appreciate a well-crafted handle. The handle of a rod is what makes or breaks the deal. A longer handled rod can be laid along the arm helping to pull against a heavy fish. And if necessary the butt of the handle can be dropped into the waistline for added strength. This is something simple but after many hours of fishing it can relieve a worn down arm. For me, the strength is in the handle.

Nothing beats a high quality fishing rod to feel every rock, bump and bite. I buy the best rod that I can afford. As I have grown as a fisherman my rod selection increased to the IM8 or high-end modulus with 64 million modulus or higher. A medium action graphite rod with a fast tip is my all around river rod. A 6-7 foot rod provides the right length to fish around others while slipping between the many overhanging trees.

REELS

When I am considering spinning reels it is all about smoothness. Good reels are smooth and last a long time. Smooth reels are often determined by the number of ball bearings inside. The more quality bearings in a reel prevent it from wobbling. Tight fitting bearings, internal gears, and external casing make a solid reel with no play in the components. There is a considerable difference between a spinning reel with only a few ball bearings to those with 10. A quality reel will house 8-10 ball bearings making it stable and allowing perfect performance.

The river can be harsh on a spinning reel, the dirty water and constant drag can harm the internal components. The higher end reels with a high ball bearing count will last much longer than those

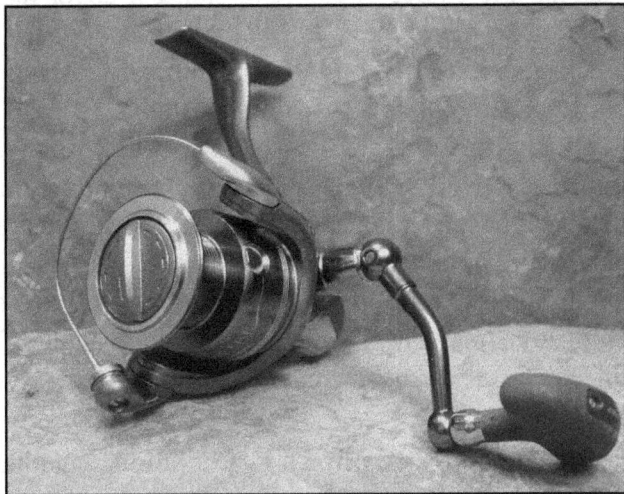

The river is very hard on reels. The constant drag, big walleye, and dirt in the gears wreak havoc.

with fewer ball bearings. The drag systems that consistently perform best are front drags. They provide constant pressure and can be adjusted easily. Rear drag systems are easier to access but often do not perform as well.

To best set hooks no backwards play in the reel is necessary. Any backward motion will cause lost opportunities. These are anti-reverse handles. Although it is nice to have the reel always stop at the top of the reel it will cause more problems in the long run. As the bail spins backwards to stop at the top it slams the gear which is very hard on the spinning reel.

Not a lot is discussed about gear ratio but this helps in the type of fishing you prefer. Common ratios are 4:1, 5:1, and 6:1. A 4:1 gear ratio means the reel will spin four times for every one turn of the handle. 4:1 are considered slow retrievers while 6:1 are for faster retrieves. This helps a fisherman who needs the reel to match his fishing style.

Lastly, match the reel's weight and size to the rod selected. This means that your lighter gear for late season fishing would be different than the heavier gear during higher water conditions. Make sure the reel holds the proper amount of line. Then make sure everything is balanced. After putting together the reel and rod I am looking for a balanced combo. If I hold the combo up with one finger in front of the reel I want it balancing, this makes fishing all day easier.

FISHING LINE CONTROVERSY

Fishing line choice is controversial. I'll cover monofilament, fluorocarbon and braided line. Luckily for us, our use of the line is for a very specific situation – river fishing. The Maumee River walleye demands strength and abrasion resistant.

For many years monofilament has been the standard for fishing line. It works great, is strong and relatively transparent. Fluorocarbon has been a newer line which has less stretch and virtually disappears in the water. Braided line has been taking the fisherman by surprise with its strength and no stretch. Each of these lines has characteristics that give fisherman an advantage. We'll discuss the differences and attributes of each fishing line.

MONOFILAMENT

Monofilament fishing line has been a long standing standard in the

Fishing line is the link between you and a trophy walleye. Quality line is worth every penny.

fishing world for years. Mono has far more stretch thus giving extra lag in the line. Compared to the other types of fishing line offered on the market today it has less feel. The benefits are the stretch characteristic provides shock absorption making it easier on fishing equipment. This provides extra time for the hook-up which helps to not pull the hook out during a hook set.

Mono is relatively easy to work with and floats in the water. This line is developed from a single fiber of plastic making it inexpensive. Remember that all fishing line is not created equal! Walleye have a harder time seeing mono especially in discolored river water. Although it is less expensive even the best mono does not last as long as braided line.

FLUOROCARBON

Submerged in water fluorocarbon becomes nearly invisible. The flu-

Warm waders help fishermen withstand the cold water. Insulated waders helped complete a limit in the frigid March water.

orocarbon's lines do not absorb water like many of the other monofilaments. It has an outer coating that cuts water much better. Fluorocarbon line sinks within the water instead of floating. Because of these characteristics it does not bow in the water the way monofilament lines do. There is less stretch then mono fishing lines. Lastly, knot strength can be a problem unless a different fluorocarbon knot is used.

BRAIDED LINE

There is a good reason braided line is also called super line. There is virtually zero stretch. These newer synthetic lines provide exceptional feeling because of the zero stretch. Along with zero stretch is higher knot strength. These qualities come at a price. Because it is tougher to develop the cost is much higher.

This line floats much more than monofilament. Braided line is abrasion resistant to stand up to sharp rocks and snags. After a lot of use there will be frayed braids towards the end of the line. Castability is very good because braided line has no memory and it has a smaller diameter. This makes it ideal for situations which require

Spring river water is cold; ensure the waders you choose are thick enough to keep you warm.

longer casts. Braided line eats away at fiberglass eyelets and can be hard on the reel. The color of the line makes it much more visible in the water, although in the past year strides have been made to develop alternate colors.

This is all great information but the real question is what should I use in the river? Everyone has an opinion and favorites; but today here is the best option. For running a Carolina rig with a floating jighead I prefer to use a 15-20 lb braided line with a tough 10-12 lb monofilament leader. I do this because I require strength for rocks and feel for walleye bites. The monofilament leader provides the floating jig a better opportunity to float while the line disappears in the water. Then during the latter part of the season when I am finesse fishing with lighter gear and tiny leadhead jigs I switch to an 8 lb monofilament for the entire rig.

WADERS

In the Maumee River waders are the main way for fishermen to access the river. Even those with boats often trade the watercraft in for waders during the spring. This is because the walleye are abundant and many great locations are within reach of the shoreline. Given this, it is important to have a comfortable and warm pair of waders.

Waders come in a variety of styles and types but I will only focus on those best suited for the cold, spring waters. Waders come in rubber, neoprene, and breathable models. Rubbers waders were common when I grew up fishing the river, but since then neoprene has been the most preferred material. Rubber waders easily leak and are colder than their counterpart. Breathable waders are wonderful for summer smallmouth fishing, but often too cold for the frigid spring waters. That leaves us with the neoprene waders which are best choice for spring fishing in the Maumee.

Chest waders are preferred but not required. I have seen many fisherman using hip waders in the channels and close to shore.

In case of an accident wader belts prevent water from filling up a fishermen's waders with cold water.

All of these varieties work well. Chest waders allow fisherman to reach the deeper waters in the main channel.

Neoprene waders generally are measured in millimeters of thickness, from 3 mm – 5 mm. A thicker 5 mm is preferred because of the added durability and warmth. You will appreciate the extra warmth during long days on the water. A few extra added items that make waders better are reinforced padded knees and a felt-soled boot. The felt soles allow for easy navigation on the pebble rocks but are slick on mud and algae. Cleats on the bottom are great on mud and algae but a bit more difficult on rocks. Some felt soles have extra cleats within the sole of the boot; this gives you the best of both worlds. Some companies make interchangeable sole systems with hefty rubber soles and sturdy spikes. These can be strapped on the boot sole to match the wading conditions. The right sole allows a fisherman to hold steady in the heavy current.

The last component is deciding the boot style, which is either bootfoot or stockingfoot. The boot style has the boot directly attached to the wader. This style is easier to take on and off but can make walking a bit more difficult because they are not snug. Stockingfoot are great for comfort because they fit perfectly and snug. Once you decide on a choice of waders get a pair of pant guards to strap around your pants and keep them down in your waders.

LIFE JACKET

The warming weather of the spring reminds me of walleye run, a great time to visit Northern Ohio. Just as quickly a fun afternoon of fishing can turn deadly. Many fishermen do not wear life jackets while fishing the river waters. It only takes seconds for an accident to happen, wear it and stay alive.

In the chart below the Ohio Department of Natural Resources has provided a detailed graph of inflatable devices from Type I through Type V. Each has a purpose and should be warn while enjoying water sports.

Type I: Offshore Life Jacket

Designed for extended survival in large, rough waters where rescue may be slow in coming, this life jacket is required on commercial craft. This type can turn an unconscious person to a vertical or slightly backward position. Unless it's inflatable, this life jacket tends to be bulky and uncomfortable in warm weather.

Type II: Near Shore Buoyant Vest

Considered the "most common" life jacket, this PFD is for use in calm, near shore waters where there is a chance of fast rescue. It is available in a variety of sizes and is less bulky and more affordable than the offshore life jacket. It will also turn most unconscious people face up in the water.

Type III: Flotation Aid

This life jacket is regarded as the "most comfortable," with a wide range of styles for different boating activities and sports. Ideal for calm water situations, this type generally will not turn an unconscious person face up in the water unless it's inflatable.

Type IV: Throwable Device

Designed to be thrown to someone who has fallen overboard, this device should be immediately available for emergencies and should not be used for small children, nonswimmers or unconscious victims.

Type V: Special Use Device

This type of PFD is designed for a specific user and can include work vest and deck suits. The device contains varying levels of inherent buoyancy and is often inflatable to provide additional flotation. Some special use devices must be worn when the boat is underway.

Lifejacket information provided by ODNR

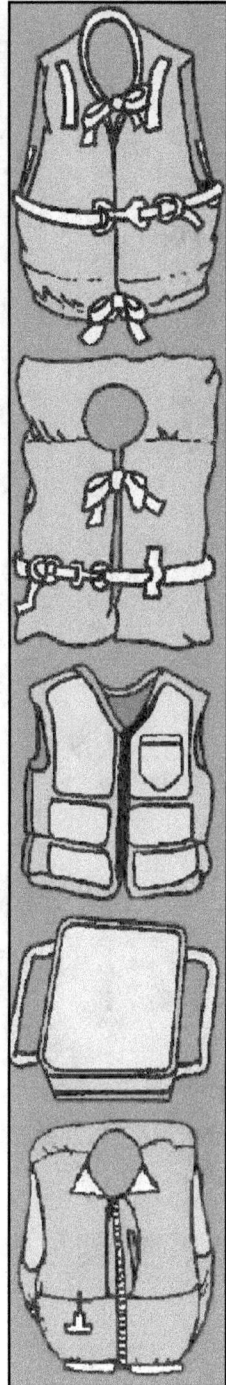

A large landing net with a short handle is ideal for scooping up large walleye while wading the Maumee River.

Aside from the different Coast Guard approved jackets there are several features that have improved usability. Many fisherman and boaters complain about the life jackets being uncomfortable and bulky. The newer inflatable models have solved this problem. There are both manual and auto inflatable life jackets. They are sleek and form fitting. The low profile inflatables make them comfortable and extremely lightweight. I have really enjoyed using inflatable life jackets over the standard foam models.

Also, during the cooler weather periods of the season float coats are a great option. They provide both warmth and the necessary safety in the rough river waters. These coats are very comfortable.

Wader belts also seem like a simple item to wear. It is an additional safety precaution. If you have the unfortunate mistake of falling into the water this belt prevents water from filling your waders. I prefer a wader belt with a plastic quick release clip for quick opening. If I needed to remove my waders quickly after falling I can click the belt open. I hope this does not happen but I would rather be safe than sorry.

While choosing a life jacket make sure it is the right type for your fishing and experience. Most people drown close to shore because they are not wearing a life jacket. The Unites States Coast Guard indicates, "It can't save you if you don't use it. Research and boating accident statistics have shown that the most frequent failure resulting in drowning is not having a PFD available when needed."

LANDING NET

Sometimes selecting the proper landing net can be an oversight. While looking for a net here are some of the features which make a great landing net for river fishing.

Starting out I want a net that attaches to my wader belt and also floats on the surface of the water. Many models float, if not adding spray foam into the handle or wrapped foam onto the front end will make it float. Additionally you need a sturdy string and clip to attach it to your body so it doesn't float away. This past year I watched a fisherman upstream land a nice walleye. In his excitement his net was released and floated downstream into my hands. Luckily I was in the right location to catch his net and return it to the rightful owner.

Walleye can range in size therefore a smaller mesh is preferred. A mesh which is coated will eliminate hooks from getting caught in the mesh, an added feature. Look for a strong hoop and handle. There should be no play in any of these parts. I prefer a short 2-3 foot handle; this gives me a little extra reach when using a long leader.

STRINGER

Day in and out a fisherman's stringer is what brings home the catch. A good stringer will last years and outperform their lesser counterparts. I know this all too well. Those who remember the years of the "ten fish walleye limit" have been fishing the Maumee River for a long time. That year, during the peak of the walleye run, I worked hard all day catching fish. Finally by late afternoon I was proud to have a limit of walleye. Packing up my gear, I turned to leave when my stringer caught on a protruding rock. The bottom ring broke and the entire limit slipped off the chain and back into the water. I was devastated with the loss after working so hard.

Secure your landing net to your wader belt to ensure it is not swept away by the current.

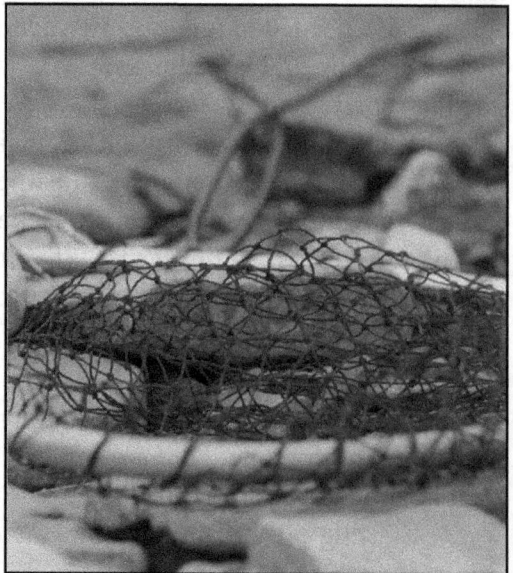

Hooking walleye through both the upper and lower jaw ensures a solid connection.

After that event I learned a high quality stringer is necessary. Newer stringers are built with cable or nylon which will not rust, rot, or break. Also I prefer locks on the clips to prevent a hook from mistakenly opening. This has happened with older stringers far too often. Lastly, looping your stringer in a circle prevents them from hanging too far away, and catching on rocks. I take the bottom hook and connect it to the top clip to complete the circle.

GADGETS

A couple extra gadgets that will make river fishing easier are fishing pliers, clippers, a hook sharpener, and a jig buster. With the many snags both in rocks and foul hooked fish, pliers are a necessity. Snags are inevitable with so many fishermen sharing the same place. Clippers will allow for tangled lines to be separated when they are too messy to untangle. The river bottom is full of hook dulling rocks. A perfectly sharpened hook will catch more fish. Polarized sunglasses are necessary to protect my eyes against flying jigs and eliminate water glair.

Is there a rod, reel or stringer that woks above all others? If you ask a dozen avid fishermen you will likely get a dozen different answers. Everyone has their own personal preference. I have used dozens of different fishing rods and reels over the years. There is not a magic spinning rod that will make fish jump onto your line. I stick with products that I know and have grown to trust. That is not to say there isn't something better. Some products are simply out of my price point so it doesn't matter how well it works.

What I like most about the spring walleye run is that anyone can partake in the sport. Fishermen can be successful using anything from the simplest tackle to the most advanced. Above is listed some of the reasons I have selected the fishing gear I use. As I have upgraded equipment, I can honestly say it has helped me catch and keep more fish. High quality equipment is proven to make fishermen more successful.

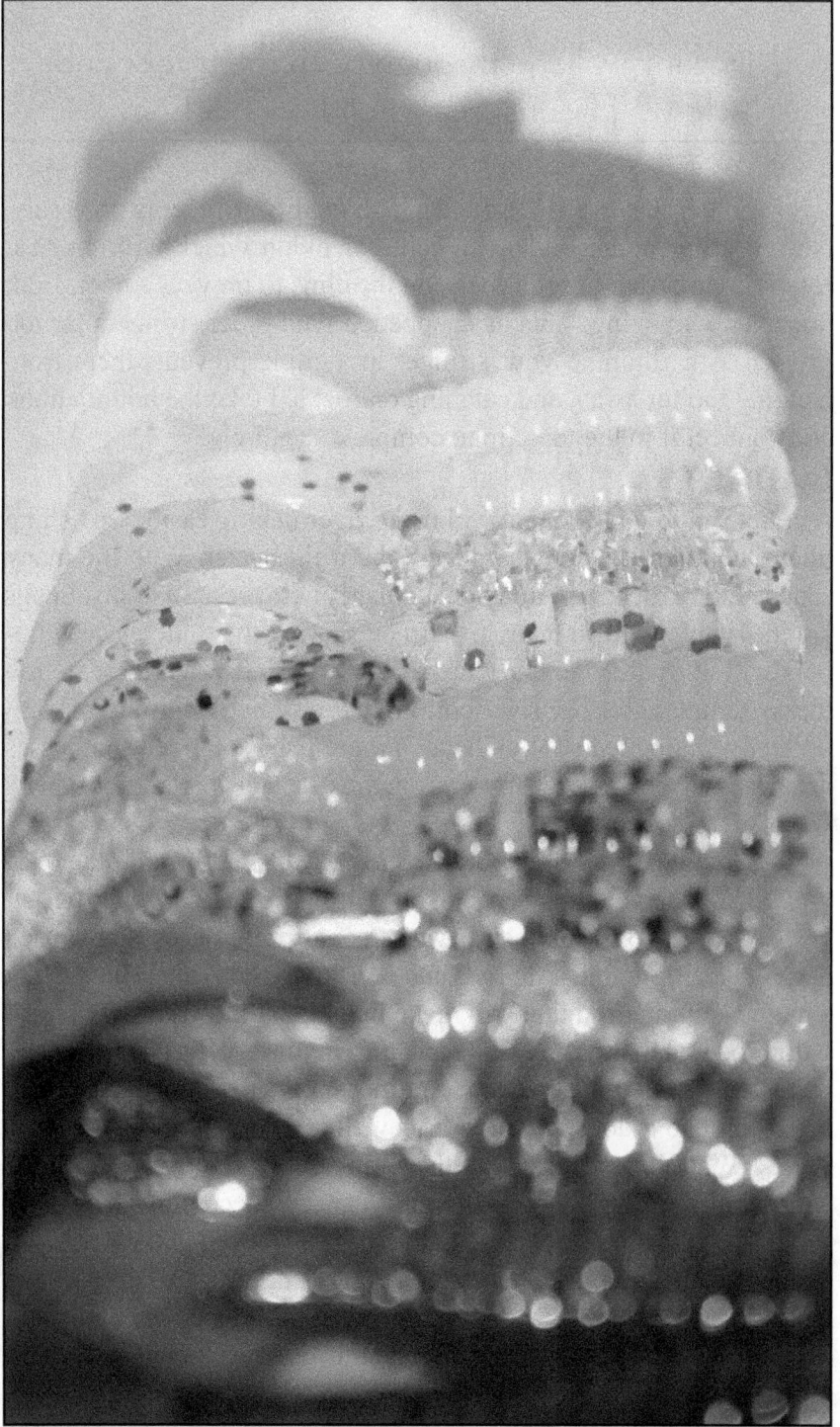

Chapter 3

Walleye Senses: Vision

As the winter months drag on, I dig out my spring walleye fishing gear to kill the winter blues. It is time again to sort through my equipment, taking inventory for the coming season. Over 25 years of river fishing experience has given me knowledge on what types of colors I use versus others. With several thousand grub tails spread out on my dining room table, my wife wonders if I'm opening a bait shop. Sitting there looking over the various lures, I quickly fall into a daydream of seasons past.

The breath of fresh air blows past me with a slight splash from the rapids. I look over the unforgettable blazing orange sun cresting the Eastern horizon. The rays stretch over the water lighting the untouched surface. Just then I am welcomed by a flock of geese flying down the river and raising their horn as if they were signaling the start of a new season. The water is cool to touch and I can see the mist rolling off the surface of the river, quickly absorbed by the cool morning air.

It's time, time to let out the first cast of the season. The excitement almost overcomes me. I am once again enjoying the natural beauty of the Maumee River. You never know what you'll see because there are so many different species of fish, birds, and animals that reside along the Maumee. Not long and the spin of the reel whistles harshly as I set the hook on a waiting walleye. My heart races and my pulse quickens as the fish dives hard into the rolling rapids. I let him run one last time before I play the fish into my hand. The fight was too short but there are many more walleye to be had.

While unhooking the fish I look closely at the bubble gum pink jig embedded into his upper jaw. Snapping back into reality I remember I was sorting out my fishing gear. But wait; I caught him on bubblegum pink? I can't imagine what walleye must be thinking to attack a lure that is bubblegum pink. There is not any baitfish living in the river that is pink or even chartreuse a popular walleye lure color? And why are so many walleye caught on colors completely unnatural to the river system?

To help understand why particular colors work better than others we must see the world through the eyes of a walleye. Although that is impossible, we can understand how walleye eyes work and what colors they see most vividly. A walleye's vision is very different than a human's. Furthermore, light conditions under water cause different colors to be viewed in different ways.

Some days lure color can make all the difference while other days it does not matter. A selection of colors ensures fishing success each day on the water.

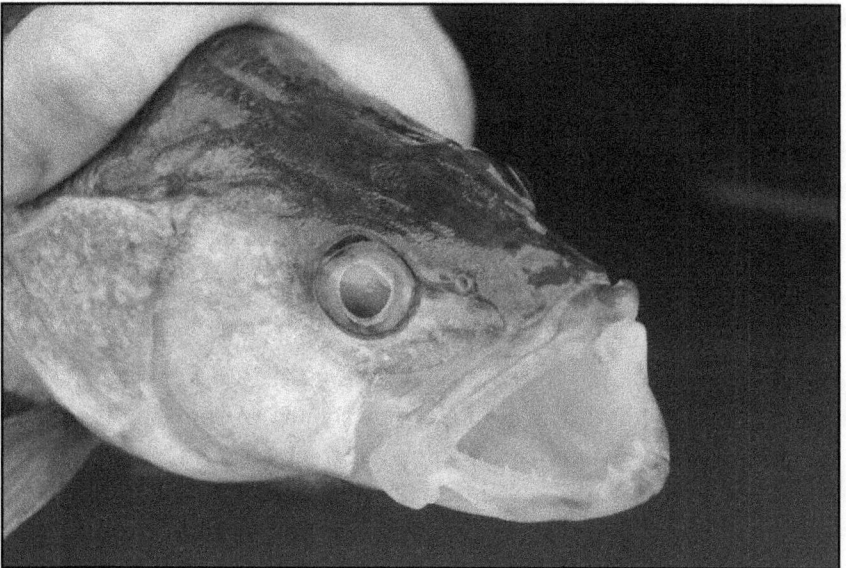

Walleye are sensitive to red, orange, yellow, and green therefore they see these colors the brightest.

Professor Dwight Burkhardt was the first to study the vision of walleye. His discoveries over three decades ago were profound on what we know about walleye vision. Through the next chapter I will discuss his discoveries and what other scientists have revealed about light conditions and color. This will help you greatly improve your selection of what color to use during the different fishing conditions.

THE SCIENCE WITHIN THE EYES

Inside a walleye's eye are both rods and cones similar to human eyes. The cone receptors are responsible for color and rod receptors are primarily responsible for greater night vision. We all know that cats have amazing night vision and this is because cats have nearly twenty-five rods for each cone. Walleye also have a high number of rods in their eyes making them have greater night vision. Also the tapetum within their eyes allow light to reflect back into their eyes for greater night vision. This tapetum is what causes walleye eyes to appear like they are glowing.

Additionally, there are two types of cones in their eyes which combine to allow the walleye to see red, orange, yellow, and green. Burkhardt's studies helped with the development of chartreuse which is the most widely used walleye fishing color today. The types of cones in a walleye's eye actually cause them to see colors different than other fresh water fish. Since walleye eyes are sensitive to red, orange, yellow, and green they see these colors in this region of the color spectrum as the brightest. Within the color spectrum of

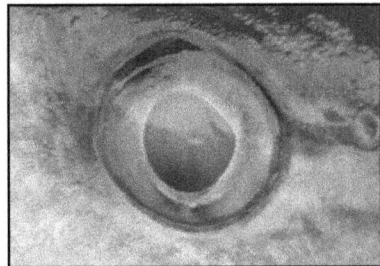

Walleye eyes are sensitive to light causing them to become active early or late in the day.

> Chartreuse is an excellent walleye color
> because it gets deep penetration
> into the water column.

red, orange, yellow, and green there are hundreds of different color shades and patterns to select.

Light looks different under water than above. And the deeper you are submerged underwater the less light you have available. Visible light can penetrate through water but quickly is diminished by light being scattered and absorbed. The more murky the water, the less light can penetrate into the depths. Murky water has a greater number of microscopic particles floating in the water. After a spring rain the river is often stained very heavily with mud and other debris limiting vision to less than one inch. Then for many days the particles of dirt are washed downstream and begin to settle. This allows the water to become less stained and clearer.

Color is a very small spectrum of wavelengths that is sensitive to eyes. The portion of the light spectrum visible to the human eye consists of wavelengths from 400 – 700 nm (nanometers), which makes up all of colors in the rainbow. Wavelengths out of this range are not seen by our eyes. Colors with shorter wavelengths penetrate deeper into the water then those with longer wavelengths. Following is the order that color disappears in water; red, orange, yellow, green, blue, indigo and violet.

BACK TO THE WALLEYE

So how does that all apply to fishing for walleye? Earlier it was stated that walleye's eyes are sensitive to the red, orange, yellow, and green part of the color spectrum. Chartreuse for decades has been the "go to" color for walleye fishing across the United States. Chartreuse is a blend between the yellow and green. Green is the shortest wavelength visible to walleye, so it gets deeper penetration than the other colors. And lastly, as indicated chartreuse is a color that walleye see the brightest. Therefore chartreuse is a great color for walleye, especially aggressive walleye.

Cutting through some more of the scientific work gets us

back to what works best under different water conditions. Although using different color lures for the right condition is a start, there are many other factors which come into play; water clarity, wall-eye temperament, weather conditions, and presentation. Many of the walleye fishermen in the river only carry chartreuse lures but when the conditions are not right they are left wondering why the fish aren't biting. And even those fishing with the perfect color for the conditions need to also pull together the right location, depth, speed, and simply feeling the bites. Picking the right color is only a piece of the walleye fishing puzzle. Actively feeding walleye can be caught on any color but when the fishing gets tough the right color can make all the difference.

In clear water a more natural presentation is favorable. Some lures that fall into this spectrum are white, pearl, clear glitter, brown, and purple. These colors are proven to work well in clear water conditions when walleye can see farther. They are less visible and more natural to the forage found in the river. In contrast, the more stained water causes fisherman to brighten up the color selection, with lures

Picking the right color is part of solving the walleye fishing riddle. This walleye swallowed a contrasting orange jighead chartreuse grub tail combonation.

Contrasting color combinations on a lure are more visible than a single color. This works with a multicolor grub tail or contrasting jighead and grub tail.

in the chartreuse, red, orange, and pink categories as better starting points. Additionally, contrasting color combinations on a lure are more visible than a single color. One of my favorite contrasting color combinations is the pink/white mix.

Even knowing which color to start with given the water clarity doesn't guarantee success. Fishing in relatively clear water in deeper holes may require brighter color presentations that penetrate better in the depths. Additionally, when the sun is high in the sky sunlight penetrates further than times with less sunlight. We have all experienced lures that shouldn't work because of water clarity and light penetration work. When selecting lure color water clarity and light penetration is a starting point to work from.

One of the ways I start my day is to put on a brighter color to catch those aggressive walleye. But once it slows down I'll switch to something that closer matches the conditions, often a silver or white color with a slower presentation. At this point I am looking to catch a few of the neutral or inactive walleye. Just because a school of fish are running together doesn't mean they all have the same temperament. Within the school some will be active, while others are neu-

Walleye forage heavily during lower light conditions or locations where light is less intense during midday.

tral or inactive. Working different colors will help you capitalize on more fish, adapting to the changing conditions.

Walleye are more active in the morning and evening hours when the sun is closer to the horizon. This angled light cuts down on the penetration into the water. Choppy water also reduces light penetration and further extends this active period. Windy days and high water which cause larger chop are ideal conditions to take advantage of active walleye for longer periods. Even on calmer days, the river always has chop but different areas of the river have larger chop on the surface. This chop results in a reduction of light and allows walleye to suspend higher in the hole for a longer period of time.

Whenever heading to the river I carry a whole selection of grub tails. Back in April 2003 I had a unique incident happen that changed the way I fish today. Like many days on the Maumee, the walleye seemed to have lock jaw. I had an opportunity to head out to the river during the midafternoon while the sun was still high in the sky. With the poor fishing conditions I had my pick of spots. That afternoon I began fishing near a friend that I often see along the shores. Knowing the water was beginning to clear from previously higher water conditions I decided it was a good chance to experiment, starting out with bright aggressive colors then quickly changing to several others. Every five minutes found me making a color change. After thirty minutes I felt a small tap on the 3" clear glitter tail tied to the end of my line. I quickly raised the rod and felt him pull tight against the line; the fun had just begun. The heavy current and few fishermen around made for a great fight as he made several runs to get away. It wasn't long before I was reaching out with my left hand to scoop him up into my net. I couldn't wait to get him onto the stringing so I could continue after another walleye. It didn't take long for the circumstances to repeat itself with another perfect walleye.

During the entire time I was carrying on a nice conversation with my friend who was struggling. There have been many times I was wearing that shoe. I told him that I felt it was the clear glitter that was making the difference. Since he didn't have any I reached into my pouch and shared a few to see if that made the difference. To my amazement after switching it only took two casts before landing his first walleye of the day. Could it have really made that big a difference? It wasn't long before we both had stringers full of walleye and shortly after I depleted all my clear glitter grubs. We both continued to fish for the next thirty minutes using many other colors. Not a single walleye struck any of those other colors. That trip solidified in my mind the importance that color has on my success as a fisherman.

The simple selection of color is important, but the depth and how that color appears to the fish is yet another factor to consider. Because walleye have a high number of rods in their eyes, they are sensitive to sunlight. Walleye have good night vision and forage more heavily during lower light conditions. But even during midday you can catch fish by working the deeper holes. The walleye which were positioned on the flats or suspended earlier in the day have often sunk deeper into the holes where light is less intense. In recent years my brother has noticed that walleye strikes on sunny afternoons come when clouds cover the sun. These can be very short but specific times to catch walleye when the conditions are not favorable.

With so much information about how walleye see different colors at different depths it's easy to get lost in the science. What I have found is these color recommendations are a good starting point. Keeping a log of what works best in different areas of the river under different conditions will help you more quickly fine tune your approach. I have a high water location where a pink/white 3" grub had been one of the best producing lures for years. Then in recent years I modified this to be a white floater and a brighter pink grub. What I thought was a great combination just got better. Don't be afraid to keep trying to improve what is already working. In this case I think the full length brighter pink color allowed the walleye to see better through the dirty high water conditions.

Looking back over my full selection of grub tails I know that each river condition calls for something different: bubblegum pink, salt and pepper chartreuse, watermelon, clear with firecracker glitter and on and on. Part of fishing river walleyes is trying to figure what color will produce the most limits and which color is going to catch the next big one. It will always amaze me that some days lure color does not seem to matter at all. On other days color can make the difference between an empty stringer and a limit of walleye. Color is just a piece of the puzzle. Lure color must be combined with proper presentation and the right location. And even then different colors will catch walleye of different temperaments. Combining everything with a favorable lure color will get you on the right track to many more walleye.

Chapter 4

Walleye Senses: Smell & Taste

Look closely at a walleye and you will see some gnarly teeth and marble eyes. Wicked looking! Walleye are predators and eating machines. Their senses are exceptional, allowing them to track down and ambush their prey. These predators attack baitfish before they are even aware of any danger. Hunting under the cover of darkness in murky river water, walleye need keen senses to catch prey. Over the next few pages, the walleye's ability to taste and smell will be explored.

Reviewing scientific studies has helped me understand why some fishing techniques work while others do not. The application of that additional knowledge has changed the way I fish today. Any fish that sinks into the depths of the water columns to escape from light must hunt by using several different senses. Walleye have exceptional night vision and a highly tuned lateral line sense. Both play a huge role in catching their prey. In addition to these two senses, their acute sense of smell also gives them an advantage in the murky waters.

THE SCIENCE BEHIND TASTE AND SMELL

Dr. Keith Jones, director of research at the Berkley Fish Research Center, helps enlighten us about the sensory capability of walleye and why they react differently to various tastes and smells. Wall-

eye have well developed olfactory senses which help them taste and smell small amounts of food. Diluted solutions of particles have been dripped into the water at hatcheries to see them follow the direction of the smell to see which small walleye are most sensitive towards. Walleye taste and smell using receptors located in their noses and the area around their mouths. Tiny molecules come in contact with the receptors and trigger a response.

The olfactory sense of a walleye is determined by the genetics of the species. Extensive research has established that some scents trigger aggressive behavior from all fish. The effect of scents relates to specific species of fish. It has been determined that some fish have a considerable difference between their taste and smell. These are unique to each fish, making particular scents an important part of the fishing arsenal.

In recent years, this research has helped with the development of specific species scents. So just picking up any spray will not cover all situations. Although walleye are primarily visual and lateral line feeders, they depend on taste and smell more than bass. Taste and smell is used once they capture and hold onto prey.

There are comparatively distinct differences between what positively affects a walleye and what negatively affects a walleye. There are similarities and unique smells that walleye respond to better than other smells. For example worm extract elicited a very positive response. Additionally, there are some smells that do not trigger any response at all. These key differences have been studied in-depth to help create soft baits specifically for certain fish species. Dr. Jones has one of the most exhaustive libraries available addressing the taste preferences of different types of fish. This science helps him identify what triggers a feeding response for each specific species. Research of taste and smell has been taking place for years and will continue to improve fishing success as new findings are made.

Over the past ten years, I have tried many different types of scents for walleye. My field results have been amazing. This was long before I began researching the topic in-depth. This experience has helped me adjust my presentation during different conditions to help increase the odds for success. Dr. Jones has proven this is not another gimmick; it is brilliant science at work.

Scent can be used to allow for a couple of extra seconds to set the hook on a finicky walleye.

Initially, one of the most overlooked aspects is human odor. Human hands by themselves produce an odor that can repel fish. This is amplified when hands have an additional substance on them, such as gas, oil, sunblock, or other foreign smells that repel fish. Captain John Tucholski from J.T. Sport Fishing Charter makes all his clients wash their hands after applying sunblock. Tucholski is actually onto something important that was proven by Dr. Jones' research, which confirmed that some ingredients in sunscreen are repulsive to fish due to several specific chemicals. These chemicals can deter fish and ruin a day on the water. Keeping hands free and clear of foreign odors is a good step in the right direction. Becoming scent-free is not just for deer hunters anymore.

In the past decade, many different types of soft baits have been introduced into the market, including salty baits, spray-on scents, impregnated baits, and even smells targeted for specific fish. Initially I was skeptical of the new gimmicks on the market. My skepticism turned into belief after reviewing the research cited earlier. Knowing that walleye have a good sense of smell, it is only logical to tie that relationship with scent baits. In all, field studies have confirmed scent play an important role in catching more fish.

To further his results, Dr. Jones has given walleye a "taste test." This consists of dropping different pellets of food, soft plastics, soft plastic with impregnated foods, and so on into a fish tank. Because walleye are extremely visual, the fish will rush over and take the pellet into its mouth. Then it will reject the pellet immediately, hold it for a sustainable amount of time, or swallow it. Often plastic without scent will be rejected immediately. Plastics with scent impregnated will be held for a few seconds, and impregnated lures with a softer permeable material or a favorably taste will be ingested. Essentially, if the walleye really likes what he tastes, he will swallow it.

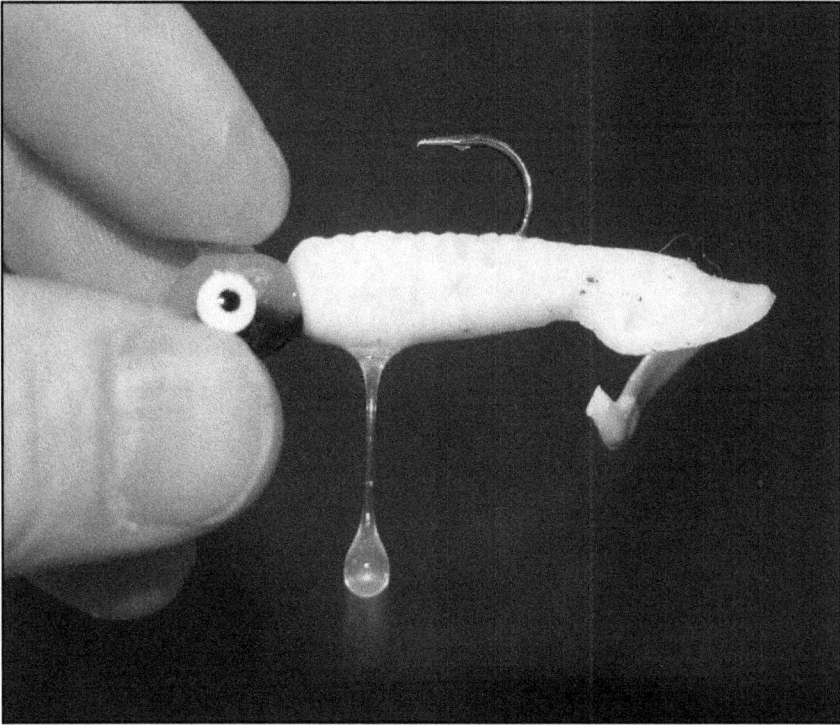

Spray on scent works well but the consistancy needs to be enough to spread in the water while lasting long enough for a dozen or more casts. Reapply often for better results.

     A walleye's reaction time to reject a food is far superior to a bass. Dr. Jones indicates walleye will reject bait lightning fast - faster than can be timed on a stopwatch.

BACK TO THE WALLEYE

Let's get back to the fishing applications and field research specific to the Maumee River. Any time your lure presentation occurs in stained water, scent will aid your success. This aligns perfectly with scoring spring walleye. Many fishermen know that tipping your bait with a minnow or worms will increase success. This is often because of the scent that is associated with the bait. While bass fishing several years ago I pounded the water for four hours without a bite. Finally I threw in the towel and loaded up a night crawler. In a matter of minutes, I landed my first fish of the day. Did scent play a factor?

I have found that higher water often prevails while river fishing in the spring. During rain storms, the rising water will fill the river with dirt making for limited visibility. When walleye cannot see to chase lures they have to rely on other senses. Any time I find inactive fish and tough conditions, I can easily attribute applying scent to an increase in success. When fishing, I am always looking for any slight advantage. Although applying scents does not double my success, it has certainly attributed to more hookups.

Hookups increase with the use of scent because walleye smell and taste through their nose and mouth. If a walleye tackles your bait, it's very likely that he will hook himself. No work needed from you. But so often while river fishing a finicky walleye lightly picks up your lure. The majority of fishermen do not realize how often they do not feel walleye do this. Scent baits play a huge role in this situation. They give you those extra couple seconds for the finicky walleye to hold onto your bait. I gratefully accept a couple extra seconds to set the hook, especially during a tough day on the water.

Over the past decade I have tried many different scents, including sprays, gels, impregnated soft bait, and salty soft baits. So what is the best scent to use? I have found impregnated baits to work very well. Spray-on scent works, but it needs to be reapplied every five to ten minutes. The scented material is designed is to slowly disseminate into the water so a walleye can detect the smell around the lure. However, the current works to wash the scent away at a quicker rate than in calmer water, so spray-on scent is not as well adapted to river use.

I have found adding scent to be most productive under tough conditions and poor water clarity. Walleye can be very finicky, so I will take any advantage I can get. Even during clear water conditions scent will provide more time to set the hook. Eliminating foreign odors and adding a species-specific scent works wonders. Next time you run into tougher conditions try adding scent to your arsenal to make those few bites turn into fish on the stringer.

Chapter 5

Walleye Senses: Lateral Line & Hearing

A walleye is a predator waiting to chase down and eat an unsuspecting baitfish. With eyes that are very sensitive to light, walleye love low light conditions. However, any fish that sinks to the depths where light doesn't penetrate must also have other senses that augment eyesight. Knowledge about walleye's lateral line sense and hearing has given me the ability to thoughtfully apply different methods; almost a scientific approach to fishing. These methods will help you change techniques when the going gets tough.

Keith Jones, Ph.D., director of research at the Berkley Fish Research Center and author, is helping develop a better understanding of fish senses. Dr. Jones is one of the most knowledgeable authorities with whom I have had the pleasure of discussing walleye senses. His years of knowledge will help you understand walleye senses beyond that of a typical fisherman. This knowledge will be invaluable the next time you are fishing the river.

Fish do not have external ears like humans, but they do have somewhat similar inner ears. In fish there are bones in the inner ear that detect sound waves. Within the inner ear, a sensory hair cell responds to sound waves within the water. In addition to their ears, they also have lateral line sense, which detects vibration on the outer portion of the walleye's body. Anything that moves in the water cre-

Walleye have an extremely sensitive lateral line sense. They can single out water pressure from different baitfish within a school.

ates a disturbance that can be detected with the lateral line.

LATERAL LINE

The lateral line sense allows a walleye to detect disturbances in the water. Even in the river where the water is constantly moving, water disturbances can be detected. This is one of the walleye's keenest senses. Walleye are hunters that rely heavily on vision and the lateral line. Because they are night hunters, non-visual senses have become greatly augmented. This is exemplified by their lateral line sense, which plays a considerable role in tracking down prey, and is their next most effective sense after their vision.

Any vibration on the outer portion of the walleye's body is detected by the lateral line sense, whether it originates from a boat prop, fishing lure, baitfish, or any other object moving in the water. This sense is used to single out different vibrations. It has been proven a walleye can single out a wounded baitfish among other baitfish in a school.

There have been inordinate amounts of scientific studies done on fish senses. These studies have led many lure companies to research how walleye respond to lure movement. The lure studies quantify how much roll, flash, and swing takes place as the lure moves through the water. Those studies and field experimentation help tune lures to provide the most desirable presentation. They are simply optimized to be fish catching machines. Today, lead jigs have endless styles that swim and move through the water differently. There are far more options available than ever before.

Your reaction is probably similar to my initial reaction. In the Maumee River, I am fishing with a jig, no rattles, no vibration, nothing. This is not true, Dr. Jones states, "Even jigs or anything passing through water will disturb the water." Any movement in water, even the slightest, creates a pressure wave. These minute disturbances can be detected through the lateral line sense.

Knowing that the lateral line sense is very effective, the use of vibration should be considered. Walleye can detect minute vibrations, which can both help and harm a fisherman. During the post-spawn period in May, crankbaits and inline spinners can be utilized to offer an alternate presentation that has not been offered in the prior months.

The lateral line sense combined with the correct color and smell makes a deadly lure. This sense helps a walleye make a final commitment to engulfing its food. When a walleye is tracking down its prey, engaging it through several different senses will work spectacularly.

HEARING

Fishing many rivers throughout the Midwest has given me many field experiences. Many of these experiences have helped me assess how sound affects fish. One afternoon, I spotted several smallmouth bass suspended in the shadows of a train bridge. I immediately began sneaking along the brushy banks to get within range. Keeping out of sight was my first challenge; the brush provided the ideal cover. Then I entered the water along a shallow sandbar so I could cast into the shadows. While entering I stumbled, making a slight splash. That was enough to make the bass sink into the depths of the water. For the next hour, they ignored my fishing attempts. Experi-

Any commotion will scare walleye from the area, boat noise is a common culprit.

ences like these have helped me learn the hard way, but these tough lessons always stick with you the longest.

Studying the biology of a fish has helped me understand how well walleye can hear. Walleye hear using a hair line cell that is sensitive to water movement. The inner ear detects sound through pressure that hits the fish's bones called otoliths, moves through the fish, and registers in the back of the brain.

Sound is a pressure wave that passes through the water. When those sound waves hit the ear it detects the pressure waves. Dr. Jones indicates, "Walleye do not have an extraordinary sense of hearing. They typically range in the 50 Hz to 200 Hz. The lowest is around 20 Hz with the highest they can hear at 500 Hz." This means they can hear low sounds, but not high sounds. The range of sound they hear is much smaller than the range humans hear (20 Hz to 20,000 Hz). So walleye can hear, but their hearing is not exceptional and they are not very responsive to sounds.

So how does walleye hearing affect the way a fisherman targets walleye? Their hearing can help or hinder fishermen. Sound has been studied in detail to understand which sound waves attract fish. The most effective companies use this information to make lures with rattles specifically targeting the range that walleye can hear. Knowing this fact helps me primarily during the post-spawn (May). Restrictions on hook size and number of hooks reduce the lure choice to primarily jigs. Those limitations are lifted in May and other fishing techniques can be used. When targeting walleye during this period, I often utilize crankbaits with rattles.

On the other hand, sounds can also disturb walleye within hearing distance. Hearing distance is dictated by the origin of the sound. Sound waves created in the air do not travel well through water, but noise created in the water can be heard for quite some distance. Boat noise is sure to scatter walleye that both hear the engine and feel the vibration. The large amount of traffic on the river often has a negative effect on walleye activity.

However, boat noise does not always have a negative impact on fishing activity. There have been a few times on the Maumee River when boat traffic in the main channel moved walleye closer to wader fishermen. There was one particular trip that stands out above the rest. Each time a boat moved through the main channel, walleye were driven close enough to the wader fisherman for those along the shoreline in waders to catch fish. I believe several of the active walleye moved to the opposite side of the channel, closer to the wader fishermen. It was almost like clockwork. Unfortunately, this type of situation occurs infrequently. Boat traffic is most often detrimental, especially in clear water under 10 feet.

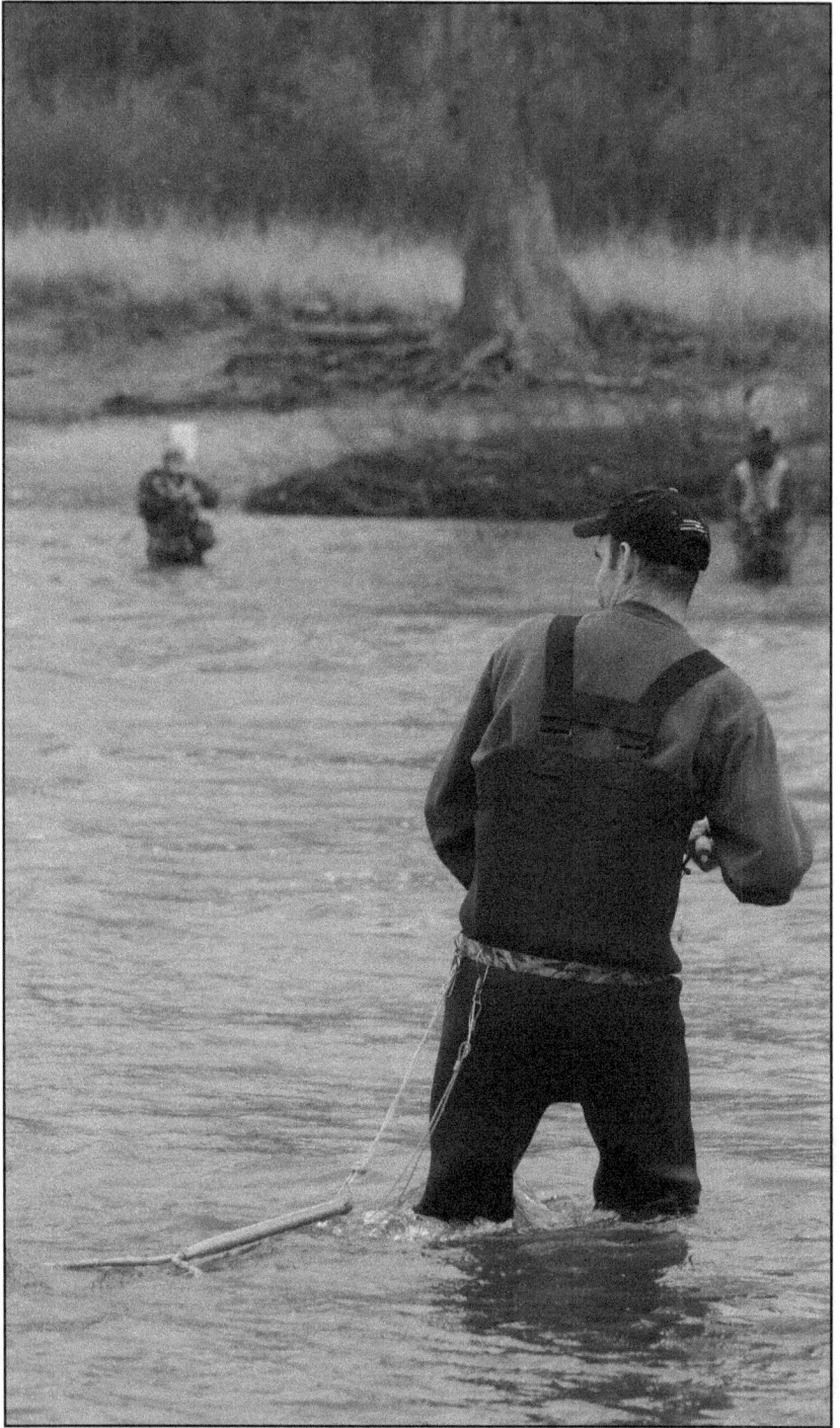

Chapter 6

Reading the Water

Observing God's power as He continues to mold and re-shape the river each year is a humbling experience. At first glance the river looks very flat and mundane. But once you take a closer look at the different ripples and calm spots, you will see that there is an entire complex and intricate aquatic world beneath the surface. The river is a world in itself with its own diverse structure; the river floor is anything but flat. Those who learn to see beyond the surface will have great fishing success.

The majority of the Maumee River is fished from the banks with waders strapped to our chest, so depth finders and underwater cameras are often not an option. And even with those technologies, being able to read the river from the surface currents and feeling structure through your rod is essential. Growing up, I fished in the locations my brother pointed out to me; I didn't understand it for myself. As the years passed I began to understand the river's terrain and reading what was beneath the surface of the ripples became easy. This was one of the turning points in my fishing career. You can show someone the door but they must walk through it by themselves. Once I stepped through that door my success doubled. And

Large debris like this entire tree floating downstream is both extremely dangerous for fishermen and will change the river structure as it drags over reefs.

once you learn to read the water for yourself then you will be able to apply your knowledge to almost any other river.

Each year the structure on the river floor changes because heavy current, large debris, and ice jams are constantly dredging the river floor. These are all perfect mechanisms to transform the underwater structure. Walking across to Blue Grass Island each year I find new treasures that are uncovered. It is always amazing to see huge trees pushed onto the island or taken downstream to another landing place. The ice jams in the spring have created tremendous damage in years gone by. Several of the tall cottonwood trees along the edge of the river have the bark torn off them ten feet from the ground. Think about the force required to create that much havoc! Even with that much fury, a majority of the river does not change, or it changes so slowly that we do not notice the differences. There are a few deep channels in the main stream that have consistently produced walleye for over twenty-five years.

Back in 2001 I was having a tough year of fishing; I couldn't consistently locate good schools of walleye. I was on a hunt traveling up and down the river; none of my "old faithful" sites seemed to be working. Part way through the season a friend turned me onto his hot location. This spot had the right combination of structure within casting distance. When no other place on the river was producing, this one held walleye. It was a tight section of rapids that caused the walleye to stack in a very specific location.

Over the years this area gained popularity so much that the rapids were stacked with more fishermen than fish. It was so good I maintained this as my "go to" spot until one year everything changed. For some reason this section of the river went dead. It was a struggle to catch fish; something was different. After some trial and error, I concluded the extremely heavy ice from the prior winter had changed the structure on the river floor. Nearby, several ancient cottonwood trees had the bark ripped off them ten feet up the tree. This type of damage on many of the trees along the river shows the amazing power of Mother Nature, and provided a clue about what had happened to my best spot.

This location held fish in a very concentrated area. I believe the heavy ice knocked over the large rocks, dredged the pebbles, and filled a better portion of the deep hole. I visited that location several times throughout the past season and noticed it still received heavy fishing pressure even though few fishermen were successful. Adapting to a new location was the right decision.

Walleye position relates closely to structure in a fast flowing river. During the spring run, walleye are continuously on the move up stream. Even with fish constantly on the move, there will be schools of fish stacking in the vicinity of structure and current breaks. The better you understand what makes up good structure for walleye and how they relate to it, the

This stringer full of walleye is the result of changing locations to find schools of walleye that were actively feeding.

Allocating time to watch others fish the river can be some of your most valuable research.

more fish you'll catch. Much of what you can learn about the river is exposed by the currents on top of the water.

The Maumee River is mature and incredibly wide. Walleye can be caught throughout the river, but the most productive spots are concentrated around great walleye structure. When I look at the river I see great spans of water with hot fishing locations dispersed among dead locations. Learning how to read the water will allow you to tell the difference between these productive and unproductive areas.

WATCH AND LEARN

In deer hunting, I have learned that actually seeing the deer you are after skyrockets your chance to later kill that deer. Walleye fishing in the river is very similar because all animals use structure in some way. The art of fishing can often be enhanced by standing back and not fishing. In today's fast paced world we have less free time than ever before. With demanding work schedules, youth soccer practices, and the rest of our family responsibilities, it is amazing we can make any time to fish. The last thing we want to do with our limited time on the river is not fish, but pulling yourself out of the water and watching others fish can be a much greater lesson than fishing yourself. When you take the time to watch other fishermen you can see their technique and what locations are producing consistent walleye. After seeing where others are catching walleye and where they are casting you will begin to see some trends.

Stand back and examine how water relates to structure. Ask yourself, what do the surface currents look like around that structure? Then, most importantly, come back during a low water period to see what the structure looks like. This practice has helped me fully understand "why" I was catching fish at specific locations during the spring run.

The best places to catch walleye during high water conditions are very different than the best low water locations. When the water is low, it is the time to scout for good higher water hot spots. Those little holes protected by a rock point which are dead during low water turn into gold mines when the water rushes high. Over the years creating a fishing log of structure helps when the underwater structure cannot be seen. Watching and learning is a great way to effectively add years of experience to your fishing expertise.

READ SURFACE CURRENTS

Fishing a new part of the river that you do not fully understand is exciting yet intimidating. Each year there is a portion of my season dedicated to chasing leads. I always have my ears open for potential hot spots. This past year was no different; I wanted to again dedicate time towards understanding some new structure. I had always been interested in the subtle current break near Blue Grass Island but had never investigated it myself. I began by doing some online research about the experiences others had. I quickly had the information needed and headed to the river, intending my venture to be solely a fact-finding mission. It was about gathering information to see if this place would accommodate my style of fishing. Instead of jumping right into the water I spent more time watching. When you are in the water you often can only see who is catching fish around your immediate location. Standing back gives you a much broader perspective. It didn't take long until I found myself searching through an old plastic container of grubs for the perfect color. Within the hour I was lugging out a stringer full of walleye. Some days it seems as if the planets are aligned making everything fall into place; this

The calm water in the middle of these rapids signifies a deeper pool of water.

Thirty years of experience reading the river currents helped Jeff Miller land his limit of walleye faster than most others on the shoreline.

was one of those days. Standing back allowed me to read the water and other fishermen. I could see the main stream of the river gave way to a subtle break in the current. As the shoreline pushed outward the main stream swept closer. This combination, along with a slight change in structure on the bottom, provided a great transitional fishing location. However, once the water depth fell below a specific height the spot was no longer productive. Lower water conditions slowed the current enough that the walleye did not prefer the location. These are slight details that can only be discovered by reading the current.

Deep holes in the river are places walleye can sink to get away from bright sun and strong river current. The Maumee River is full of drop-offs and ledges; both are deeper locations where water pools into a hole. These locations are some of the easiest to find: look for calm spots on the river surface. So if you see a spot in the river's current that looks flatter than the ripples around it, this typically signifies a deeper hole. Holes come in many shapes and sizes, from long deep channels carved into the floor of the river to small

There is a subtle current break running horizontally in this stretch of river. There is a slight change in wave height that illustrates the change in current between the sections of river.

isolated ovals. Look for the littlest calm eddies; they may only be two feet wide but very long. There are many parts of the river channel that are narrow but very deep. Other times a big round oval will be apparent. Towards the head (upstream side) of the hole, water circles around while at the tail (downstream side) of the hole the water begins to move faster. Each hole has its own characteristics, but many of them are outstanding fishing locations.

Current breaks are another place walleye can escape the strong current, and can be found in many different forms throughout the river. A majority of the better current breaks are close to shore. You can see these locations by watching where fast moving water is running right next to slower current. Often there are larger faster waves next to a calmer section with smaller ripples. When the river breaks around a wing dam or a structural point in the river, the main current extends farther into the middle of the river. These spots offer walleye places to sit on the edge in the calmer water. Break lines are located in every location up and down the Maumee River. Some of the major current breaks are caused by islands, bridge pillars, wing dams, rock points, and slight bends in the river. Locating them is part of the art of reading the surface currents of the water.

Large rocks sticking up in the water can be found by looking for the disturbance of water rushing over the structure, called a boil. Lying behind the structure is a calm section that provides a break

Rocks of this size can be found throughout the river. The calm water that lays behind them is sure to hold a few walleye.

from the current. Although small, these locations can be fantastic. The Maumee River's rocky bottom has a variety of larger rocks distributed across the river's floor. Each piece of structure provides an escape from the heavy current, allowing walleye to conserve energy. You will never actually see most of these rocks, and unless you can read the water you would never know they existed.

At times you will see places where the water is flowing back upstream. This doesn't seem possible but near the shoreline eddies are created where the water recirculates. You'll be able to see the calmer water flowing back upstream, or the surface will look calm. At times, you'll see some bubbling in the water. This upstream flow brings food back around for a second chance. Places that circle back too much collect garbage and become unattractive to walleye.

Larger expanses of riffles are always an attractant. The speed and height of the ripples are very uniform through most of the riffle. As the water flows off the rocks the water bounces rather quickly over the surface causing the disturbance. Inside many of these riffles there will be boils and slick areas. The boils signify larger rocks while the slick areas are caused by deeper pools. Look hard at the ripples for any slight change in the size of the ripples, which signifies a change in depth or bottom structure. This change will create an edge for the walleye to congregate around. The area of ripples has to be assessed for depth. Areas that are too shallow do not provide good places for walleye to gather. I prefer these areas to be several feet deep before attempting to fish.

As wide as the Maumee River is, it still winds its way out towards Lake Erie. Several of the outer edges of the curves offer the deepest part of the channel. Water moves more quickly there, drawing food into these deeper sections. The edges offer the faster current and an ideal location for ambushing a walleye. This will be seen as a calmer surface where the pool gets deeper. One of my favorite areas has a large section of ripples stretching across the inner part of the bend. Then towards the midway point the water calms down while it drops into a deeper pool of water. Working the inner edge of that pool provides an exceptional transition point.

There are also large sections of the river that seem boring and flat. As the river widens and depth increases, surface currents are not noticeable. This does not mean the area is devoid of structure if it is not causing a change in the surface. Not every location can be understood from the surface current. A good pair of polarized glasses will help look below the surface. The rest will have to be felt using a sensitive rod and high quality fishing line.

Each year I love to get back down to the river to see what has changed. The raging river gets beat up each year by rushing flood waters, chunks of ice crashing into the shore and grinding along the riverbed, and full grown trees being ripped from the ground and pushed downstream. All of these amazing transformations happen throughout the year; they are part of the river's amazing life cycle. Once you learn to read the water to interpret the results of these transformations, you can take these lessons onto any river system to catch a variety of fish.

Chapter 7

Structure

I can remember standing near my older brother in the cold murky waters of the Maumee when I was a kid. Our fishing location was a deep muddy hole on Blue Grass Island. There was something about that hole that excited me every time I cast a lure into its watery depths. It was the constantly changing fish, the opportunity of a giant fish, and the familiarity of the location.

Hundreds of locations that provide killer walleye structure is spread throughout the river system. During my younger years I focused on that one location, only because I knew it intimately. Today is a different story. Throughout my fishing career I have come to understand walleye behavior at a much deeper level, providing me a range of structures to fish. Each type of structure provides something unique that a walleye needs to survive.

River systems pose a unique challenge for the fisherman, with water level, flow, and structure constantly changing. Once you understand how and where walleyes hide, you can focus on catching them regardless of the location and condition. This holds true for any species: understand how the fish relates to the river's structure and you can concentrate your efforts on the most productive spots to catch that fish.

DEEP POOLS

I will admit it: I am a river rat from Northern Ohio. I love to fish for anything with scales and a few things without. Growing up on the banks of the great Maumee River will turn you into a fishing fool. Cutting your teeth on some of the best holes in the river will spoil a fisherman.

While still young in my fishing career, I can remember heading to my favorite holes one morning before track practice; I wanted to capitalize on the time I had to do some fishing before reporting to school. The morning was crisp and the high water pushed me back into the brushy shoreline. That morning the small hole right near the bank was loaded with walleye. It did not take long for my leadhead to sink deep into the hole where a hungry walleye could swallow up a jig head. In the bottom of the hole a huge walleye ate my lure. The rod bent over as I pulled in the heavy fish and grabbed it. My heart was racing and it only got worse once I realized I just landed a 29.5 inch walleye. Leaving the river I was at blissfully happy. My addiction was feed.

A deep pool is signified by the calmer water on the surface of the water. This one has some bubbles accumulating at the top of the water.

Walleye will stack in very specific locations within a deep hole. This graph signifies the three most common locations; suspended at the head of the pool, deep in the bottom, or at the tail of the hole. The head of the pool offers slack water and food rushing past. Many walleye hug bottom of the deep pools. At the tail of the pool the water begins to lift upward and increase in speed. (Current is moving from right to left across the diagram.)

Time after time of catching limits of walleye has given me the expertise of relying on the many holes and drop-offs. Look across the river and you see them littered in every portion of the river. But not all holes are created equal; you need to learn which produce and which do not.

Initially, look for a deep hole near the main current and there are likely to be a number of walleye hiding in the depths. Walleye love to hang in and around these deeper holes. This allows them to suspend off the edge of the drop-off waiting for prey to float past them in the faster current.

The key to fishing a deep hole is to fine tune the fish location within the hole. At any location there is a need to find the actual spot which holds the walleye. Within the drop-off you'll need to pay attention to whether the fish are on the bottom or suspended. Even further, they may prefer a specific side of the hole over another. Experimenting with different weights and leader size will be necessary to successfully catch them. Walleye don't want a lure to come zipping by at light speed. Although I don't like tossing heavy baits, you often have to use this technique in locations with faster current.

Floating jig heads inherently float up to catch suspended fish. Running a lighter inline sinker will allow the jig to sink slower into a hole. When your bait drops off the edge you will feel a void as it floats through the hole. This is a perfect situation because you are presenting the lure to suspended fish. Increasing the weight will make the lure fall more quickly, presenting the lure to fish closer to the bottom. Different leader lengths will also increase or decrease the column of water that you are fishing. These details are important when fishing such locations.

Light penetration and walleye mood will have a determining factor to their location. When light penetration is minimal walleye will be active and suspend off the edge of the drop-off. This will often occur early and late in the day. When the sun is highest light penetrates deeper into the water and walleye sink deeper into the hole. Often these walleye are less active. When this occurs a heavier sinker will drop your lure into the depths of the hole. It is so important to present your lure where the fish are positioned; lures falling above or below will result in missed opportunities.

MAIN CHANNEL

Many main channel depressions run through the river. These can be fished in the same manner as deep holes. Through the river there are different channels running through the river, some portions of the river can have several channels in parallel. The main channel edges are the focus areas for a walleye fisherman. These edges encompass some of the deepest and best holes within the river system.

When the water levels fall to normal, fishermen can wade throughout the Maumee. This gives fishermen the ability to reach those main channel edges. I have often found a particular edge of the channel holding fish. This past April while fishing off Blue Grass Island there was a line of fishermen standing on both banks. The timing was right but the fish had become tight lipped overnight.

After working the inner edge of the channel for a portion of the morning without a bite it was time to make something happen. Instead of working downstream I began searching high and low for

In the center of the river there are long deep holes referenced as deep main channels. This is a crosscut of the river looking downstream. Walleye sit deep in the bottom of the channel and also on the ledge. The sides which have several shelves at different depths hold more walleye then those which drop straight off. This picture signifies walleye located in the bottom and on the shelf before dropping into the deeper channel.

active fish. Shortly into the searching process I began casting to the farthest edge of the main channel. This was an extremely long cast but almost immediately I was hooked up with a walleye. The outer edge of the channel was holding the active walleye. I continued working the outer edge looking for a pattern. They were suspended three or four feet off the bottom where the current broke because of the deeper channel. Fish were now clinging to the farthest edge of the main channel. Days like this remind me to work every portion of the area before moving to a new location.

CURRENT BREAK

You must understand current breaks before you will be able to capitalize on the amazing fishing they offer. Looking across the river, there will be a current break where the main current and the slower water meet. There is often a larger ripple right along the edge.

The strong current creates a distinct current break that is visible by the large waves next to much smaller waves.

Current breaks, where fast moving water is running right next to slower current, can be located up and down the entire river. Walleye position themselves in slack water close to fast moving water, waiting for an easy feast. Walleye can quickly ambush their victim then retreat back to the slower current, allowing them to use as little energy as possible.

Current breaks can be caused by a number of different types of structure: points, large boulders, islands, drainage, bridges, changes in bottom structure, or changes in depth. Some of the best current breaks are created by points and large rocks. Reading this water becomes easy when you look at the size of the ripples on the surface of the water. You'll see slower small ripples next to faster large ripples, or even better, calmer water with little to no ripples next to large ripples.

Some of the times current breaks become the most pronounced is when the water is in a transitional phase, 2 to 3 foot above normal levels. When the water rises further, the main stream becomes extremely fast. Rocks that protruded above the surface in

Placing a lure near structure holding walleye is a huge step in the right direction.

low water periods give enough depth and breaks to hold fish during high water periods. Even the slightest structure creates much calmer water. These breaks can be positioned very close to shore.

When fishing the current breaks I focus on the very edge of the break. With a sweeping motion, keep the lure on the edge of the current break as long as possible. I tend to work the top of the current break initially, looking for active fish. Then I work a break down along the edge. Not all current breaks are created equal, so continue to look for the best producing areas. Just because it looks good doesn't mean it will hold fish. Continue searching for active feeders in the school of fish.

EDDIES

Walleye are opportunists. They have a knack for hanging back until something good comes floating past. What better location then an eddy of water? It's like being in a whirlpool where food circles back around them several times. There are several places on the river where the water circles back around a point or above some rapids. You'll be able to see the calmer water flowing back upstream. This upstream flow brings food back around, giving the walleye a second chance.

As water levels change there will be eddies that quickly appear then disappear just as quickly. Many of the most productive eddies I have fished only hold fish for a short period of time when the water level is just right. Shoreline features that are exposed become engulfed in water, creating many eddies that offer a break from the fast flowing water. Over the years I have found subtle eddies to be the most productive.

During higher water you will see eddies with lots of debris packed up next to the shore. Often I find when there is a tremendous amount of junk the location is either dead or full of carp. On the other hand, there is another eddy near Blue Grass Island that I find

As the water rushes past the point of rocks on the right, the water circles back around to form an eddy. Walleye stack on the front edge near the point and on the back of the eddy in the calmer water. There is a deeper pool of water that makes for an excellent hide out.

quite productive. It is very subtle and unless you're standing close to or in the river you wouldn't notice it. This slower water pools up and provides a calm location for walleye to rest before challenging the next set of rapids. At times you'll see some bubbling in the water. Although subtle, these areas should be added to the hit list.

Shoreline bends or protrusions also create pockets holding fish. Most often eddies offer less current so downsizing is necessary. Running a lighter jig allows the lures to move properly through the circling water. Make sure to search through the entire section to catch all the walleye resting in the water. This slower water is ideal for catching fish throughout the day. After fish settle down to rest from the morning move, they can be found taking a break while filling up their bellies.

ROCK PILES

There is nothing like the rocks to get you excited about walleye fishing. Millions of walleye swim upstream because the river provides

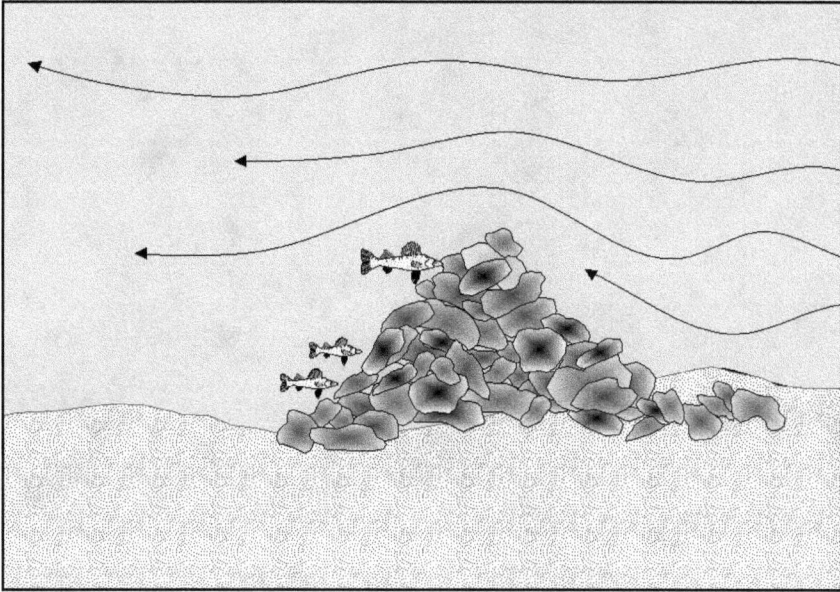

Walleye will position themselves at the top and behind the rock pile. Some of the biggest walleye sit right on the top of the rocks.

the perfect mix of structure for spawning. This type of structure goes hand in hand with walleye fishing. Simply thinking about hitting the rocks with some jigs gets me excited.

Rock piles and humps are an overlooked attribute in the river. Some of the best rock piles I fish hit their prime during higher water periods. Many of these are piles of rocks surrounded by a soft bottom. This makes them exceptionally attractive because the structure changes drastically. Walleye will sit on the front and back sides of the rock pile. Most often the larger walleye are found on the front side of the rock pile. Hitting these locations takes precise casting to bounce a jig over the front and then onto the back side of the rock pile. The walleye tend to congregate in groups, and finding the perfect spot on the rock pile is often necessary to catch fish. Once you find the exact location you will be in for a great ride.

SCATTERED ROCKY FLOOR

Along with rock piles, there are sections of rocky bottom with stacks and clumps of bigger rocks scattered along the floor of the river. These areas make great riffles in those shallower areas but scattered

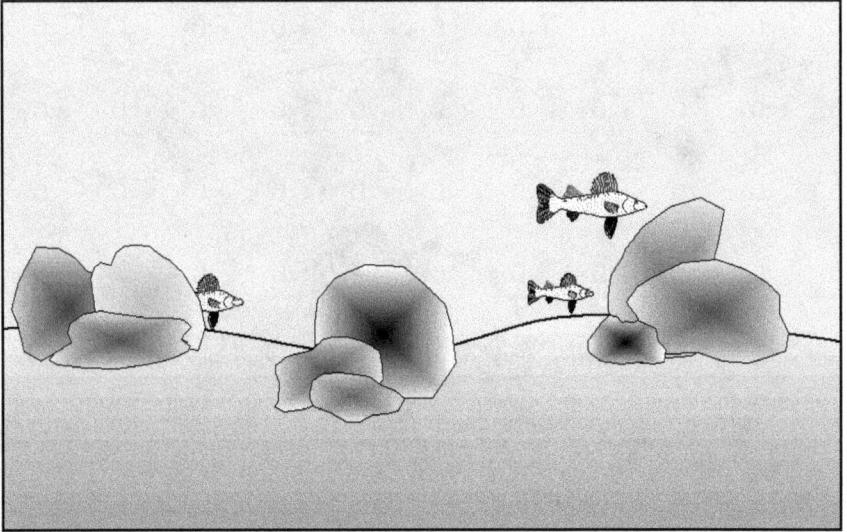

Walleye love to sit right on the floor of the river between rocks. This location can be an area littered with rocks.

rocks in deeper water are better locations for walleye to hide. Fishing a rock bottom that has some rip-rap or larger rocks can be a challenge. Bottom-hugging walleye can be difficult to fish anywhere, but add tough rock structure and the challenge increases even more. Fishing locations such as these means losing jigs, but the payoff can be great if you are willing to sacrifice a few.

Walleye love to hold tight between rocks on the river floor. These areas are best when they are directly adjacent to deeper water. During higher water periods these locations are ideal when they are closer to a current break. With rocky structure it is critical to put the lure within inches of the walleye's nose. Rocks can limit the visual range of a walleye to a few inches. Getting a jig between the rocks is the hardest part of the game, with the added difficulty is your jig bouncing around multiple rocks. The sharper rocks will cause hooks to quickly dull and the abrasion to fishing line can cause line breaks. Inspect both often to keep your gear in order.

LONE ROCKS

Smallmouth fishing the many tributaries across the Midwest has taught me great lessons about lone rocks. It does not matter if it is submerged or jutting out of the water, structures like these provide

a current break on the back side. The Maumee River provides many big rocks that point up providing ideal hiding locations. Many of these can be seen as the water rushes over them, distinguished by a disturbance where water flows over the structure. During higher water conditions you will never see most of these rocks. But as the water recedes the larger rocks begin to peek out of the watery depths. Hidden behind these locations there is always a pocket of calm, recirculating water.

Walleye will stack behind lone rocks resting from the heavy current. These locations do not have to be in shallow water. Some of the best hideouts are located within the deeper channels and holes along the river.

BRIDGE PILINGS

The bridge pilings scattered through the river can provide some good fishing. When bridge pilings are set, there is often some rip-rap scattered at the base of them. As the water hits the front of the piling it separates and provides a calm eddy behind the structure, much like a larger rock. I have found these areas to be good until the water level increases and the speed of flow is too fast. At these times the current is too fast to hold walleye behind the bridge pilings.

Casting a jig directly behind the bridge piling will let it drop quickly into the calm water.

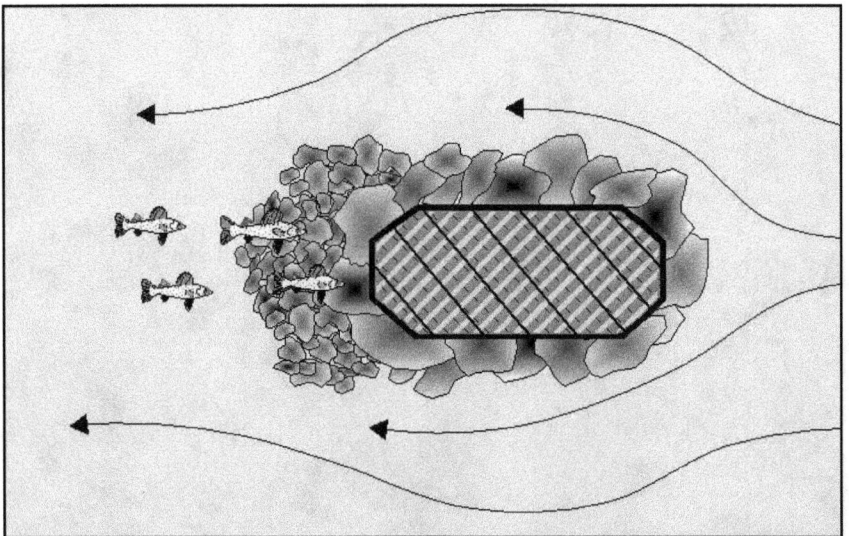

When the water speed is just right, placing a jig directly behind the piling is ideal. Don't be afraid to use a heavier leadhead to set it right down on the bottom. With too light of a weight the jig will flow out of the calmer water before the fish has a chance to strike.

RIP-RAP

The shoreline is full of rip-rap along the White Street access and stretching up the river bank from the access. Rip-rap was designed to protect the shoreline from erosion. These broken rocks, paving demolition material, and concrete help guard against the ever-flowing water. This is especially important during flood stages when the river rises and the current beats hard against the fragile shoreline. The White Street access is not the only area with rip-rap along the river.

During the higher water stages the flow of the current forces many of the walleye to seek refuge against the current. It is not uncommon to find walleye stacked right up against the banks. First

This shoreline of rip-rap protects the shoreline from erosion and provides great fishing during higher water periods. There are many stretches just like this along the river.

88

thing in the morning fish will be congregated close to shore and will eventually move outward into the deeper pockets as the morning progresses.

RIFFLES

The riffle is a very important section within the river system. These are the sections of the river that are relatively shallow but have a great amount of turbulent water pushing over the rocks. This unique portion of the river provides a place for the walleye to spawn. I have often avoided fishing the riffles because when the walleye are spawning it is very tough to get them to bite. During the peak of the spawn there will be fish rolling up on these areas. Often you will be able to see them just below the surface of the water if the clarity allows.

WING DAM

A wing dam is a barrier created to extend partway into the river. These are created to redirect current towards the center of the river. Wing dams can be both above and below the water. As the current is redirected towards the center of the river an eddy is created on the back side of the dam. These slower waters are ideal locations to find

Often water is covering the wing dam but the main current is pushed towards the middle of the river. Walleye stack behind the dam and in the eddy of water that circles behind the dam.

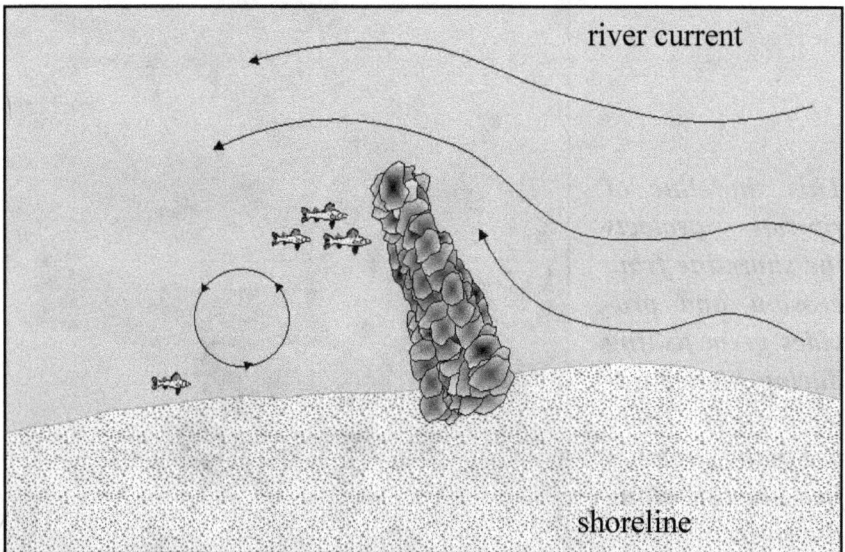

river current

shoreline

Understanding how walleye relate to structure within the river system enables a fisherman to catch walleye regardless of water levels and weather conditions.

larger female walleye staging. Work a large area when fishing on the back sides of these dams because walleye will often sit along the current break farther off the dams.

The year the new Conant Street Bridge was built, its construction and Mother Nature combined to create a perfect storm during the spring walleye run, with a fury of fishing action that has not been matched since. During that particular year two huge wing dams were built to help erect the new Conant Street Bridge. That was fine, but then as luck would have it there were a number of rain storms that created high water for a majority of the spring spawning season.

With this much water rushing downstream the wing dams provided a great amount of flow pushing through the main stream of the river. I believe the force of this flow kept a number of walleye from moving upstream past the wing dam. This caused a huge number of walleye to stack below the wing dams. On top of that, it provided high water in the lower portion of the river during the entire season, and because high water stayed for long periods, many fishermen began understanding how to fish the lower portion of the river. Needless to say, fishermen were stacked on top of each other. With the fishing ground extremely minimized because of high water and the exceptional fishing, there were people waiting on shore for others to limit out.

There are days that I catch a limit in less than thirty minutes every year. But it is rare to have this occur time after time. Changing river height, water temperature, and fishing pressure do not allow for patterns to stay the same for long periods, but that was the year that it happened: The Wing Dam Year.

CREEK INLET

Creek inlets offer new life to the river. There are a few of these hidden treasures sprinkled along the shoreline. The creek washes new food into the river. Creek beds are full of sand, and the wash-out area transitions to a rocky pebble. Often there is a drop-off that can hold walleye where the creek opens into the river. I particularly enjoy fishing them during higher or transitional water because wall-eye tend to like the area where the sand from the creak transitions to the rock along the river floor. The muddy washed out area also makes a depression. This deeper area is to shallow and slow during lower water periods. Once the water rises the water level becomes right and more current pushes into these areas. This combination of events turns a no fish zone into a great little honey hole.

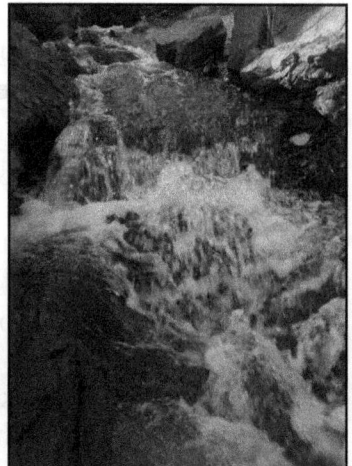

Many creeks are not as distin-guished as this one. Slow flowing ditches connecting to the river are just as productive.

ISLANDS

Topographical maps of the river show the many islands scattered throughout the river. Many of those are in the portion of the river that is the spring spawning grounds. Many fishermen are already familiar with Blue Grass Island, but there are many more islands scattered about the river.

Learning to fish island structure can be a key ingredient for success. Often islands combine a number of features that work together to provide some of the best fishing around. I was first turned on to working structure around islands while fishing for feisty smallmouth bass. The island provided a current break and a long finger reef extending off the back end. The reef side quickly dropped into deeper water and was a killer location to find a large number of big fish. Often while targeting smallmouth bass, hungry post-spawn walleye would gobble up my inline spinner.

As the water rushes across these locations, walleye will hang on the back side of the reef. The better locations are those with reefs and deeper pools on the back side. Also along the edges of the island where the island cuts back in creates an eddy where the water recirculates. Points of structure can also create an eddie where the water has a chance to circle around.

To work the back end of the island by standing behind the island working the reef without disturbing it. Cast onto the reef edge and work along the deep edge of the pool. There will be a current break downstream from the island often parallel with the reef. During higher water stages walleye will push farther up over the island and into the timber. Fishing for walleye in the timber is tough but a challenge I love. Watch the current break and how it rolls over into the deeper water. Work this entire edge for walleye resting in the slack water.

THE FLATS

The flats are what I call the less defined structures on the river. You'll look across the water and it is seamless and boring. The ripples don't change and many view this as flat and fishless. But over the years I have found this to be anything but the truth. Sometimes during the heavy fishing pressure of the walleye run those small overlooked areas provide great action. The flats are not really a structure, but they do comprise a large portion of the river. I do not want anyone to overlook these sections because they appear to be calm and featureless.

Walleye don't require a large change in the current to congregate. A small ledge of six inches might be enough, or even the change from sand to gravel could cause the fish to linger in a location. These are the types of spots that you have to find by trial and error; the places many old timers go when the rivers are flooded with people or the bites get tough to find. You really have to memorize these locations or write them down in a log book, but don't overlook them.

I learned my lesson the hard way many years ago. I noticed a lone fisherman hundreds of yards away from the crowd for days on end. He was fishing in one of those seamless locations. There was no structure I could see, and he was fishing on top of the rapids. I thought to myself that he was either crazy or didn't like crowds. Why would he isolate himself and not catch any fish? After about a week my curiosity finally got the best of me. I had to find out what was going on. And man did I ever find out! For the next five days I found myself returning for limit after limit of red-hot action. Don't think that fish are being caught just because there is a crowd. Dare to be different.

Once the surface currents of the river get calm it's very hard to fish. Unless you can locate some structure that underneath the flat surface you will not have much success. There is a stretch of water like this under the I-475 bridge. This area is often void of wader fishermen because of the deeper water but fishing this area from a boat is a completely different story.

CONCLUSION

Targeting river walleye is a structure game to me. I envision structures in the water and their effect on the river's flow like a kind of topographical map of the river. Before I even set foot in the water I am deciphering the best hiding spots for walleye, much like I use a topographical map to decipher the best game routes before I ever step into the woods when I am hunting. Solving the river's puzzle excites me because I have to use every tool at my disposal: bouncing lures to feel the bottom, reading the surface current, and even using depth finders to see beneath the surface. This is all part of the challenge of locating the most active game fish in the river.

Many of the features described above combine to make an even better location. For example, a deep pool with a several large boulders on the bottom or along the edges makes this location even better than either feature would be on its own. This is when locating the spot within the spot becomes even more important. Take the knowledge that you gained in the past few pages to help boost your own walleye fishing success.

Chapter 8

Jig Fishing Techniques

Jigs are one of the most universal and productive lures available for river fishing. They are the staple for the walleye run; nothing else works as well under those unique conditions presented by this type of fishing. Thousands of fishermen line the banks of the river each using the same setup: a jig. At the same time, the spring weather offers a variety of weather conditions. Torrential downpours overflow the river into the flood plains, and then a short week later the murky water turns crystal clear while the river recedes. At these extremes and at all the points in between, the jig remains the best lure on the river. Given this fact, understanding how to use a jig to its fullest capacity is essential to your fishing success.

You might think there is nothing new about jigs; after all, they have been used on the river long before I began fishing. I would agree that jigs have been around for centuries, but there have been so many different designs developed in the past 20 years it has become a new lure. There are many different lead head styles that swim through the water making different presentations, and the use of a jig can be adjusted to offer countless different presentations. All of these slight adjustments make it one of the most versatile lures available.

FLOATING JIGS

Before discussing how to use a floating jig, you must learn how to select the right jig for the situation. Starting out, I cannot stress enough; select a floating jig with a quality hook. Floating jigs are often built with lightweight flexible hooks to make them lighter. However, a strong stiff hook is necessary when fishing the rocky bottoms presented in the river. A hook that will not bend outward or sideways shows the needed strength and durability for the river. A thicker, quality hook holds its point well against the hard rocks, allowing for better hook sets. Also, durable hooks will not bend or break when reeling in a big walleye in the heavy current.

The hook within the floating jig comes in a variety of sizes, typically #4, #2, and #1/0. Hook size often follows the size of the float. I prefer a mid to large hook most often; a #2 hook is perfect it offers a longer shank and a wider gap which translates to better hook-ups. I feel a #4 hook is generally too small to use during the main run, and would only recommend this smaller size when finesse fishing. #1/0 hook is a good size when 3 inch grub tails and are working. Floating jigs with a collar hold the grub tail secure; those without tend to allow the grub tail to slide down the shank. Floaters without a collar are designed to use live bait while collared floating jigs are intended for grub tails. Using or not using a collar is a personal preference, but if given the choice I would take a floating jig with a collar.

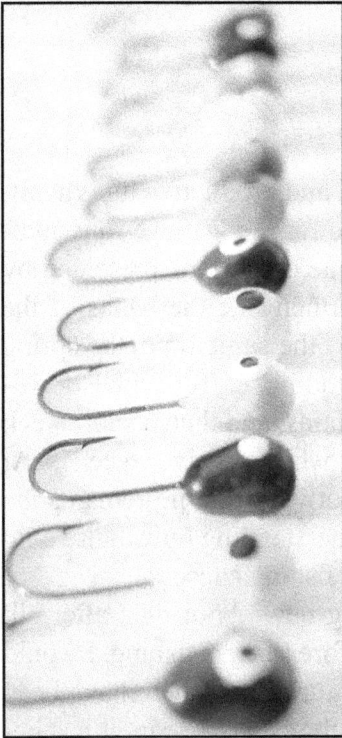

Floating jigs are most often fished with a Carolina rig. A traditional Carolina rigged floater has a leader, swivel and weight that slide

A variety of floating jig head colors allows a fisherman to provide contrasting color presentation.

Proper leader length controls how high a floater suspends in the water column. I have found longer leaders have increased my success with finicky walleye.

along the line. Most fishermen using a Carolina rig are using bullet weights, but lately fishermen have been modifying the Carolina rig with inline trolling sinkers instead. These have been very popular because of their snag-free nature. Using a fixed or sliding weight changes the resistance a fish feels when striking. Bullet weights allow the walleye to run without the weight of the jig because the line slides through the weight. This moves through the rocks easily but turbulent current can cause minor tangles as the line spins around the weight. In contrast, an inline sinker is connected directly to the line; therefore the fish feels the weight when striking. Using an inline sinker is not a true Carolina rig since the weight is not sliding. Inline weights pull through the rocks very easy with few hang-ups. These are very simple to use but are slightly more expensive. Both are valuable options to use in the river. I stay away from attaching split shot sinkers because they damage the line and slide too easily.

Floating jigs are wonderful at placing the lure above or directly in front of the fish. One of the main uses is targeting suspended walleye off the edges of drop-offs. Imagine a walleye suspended

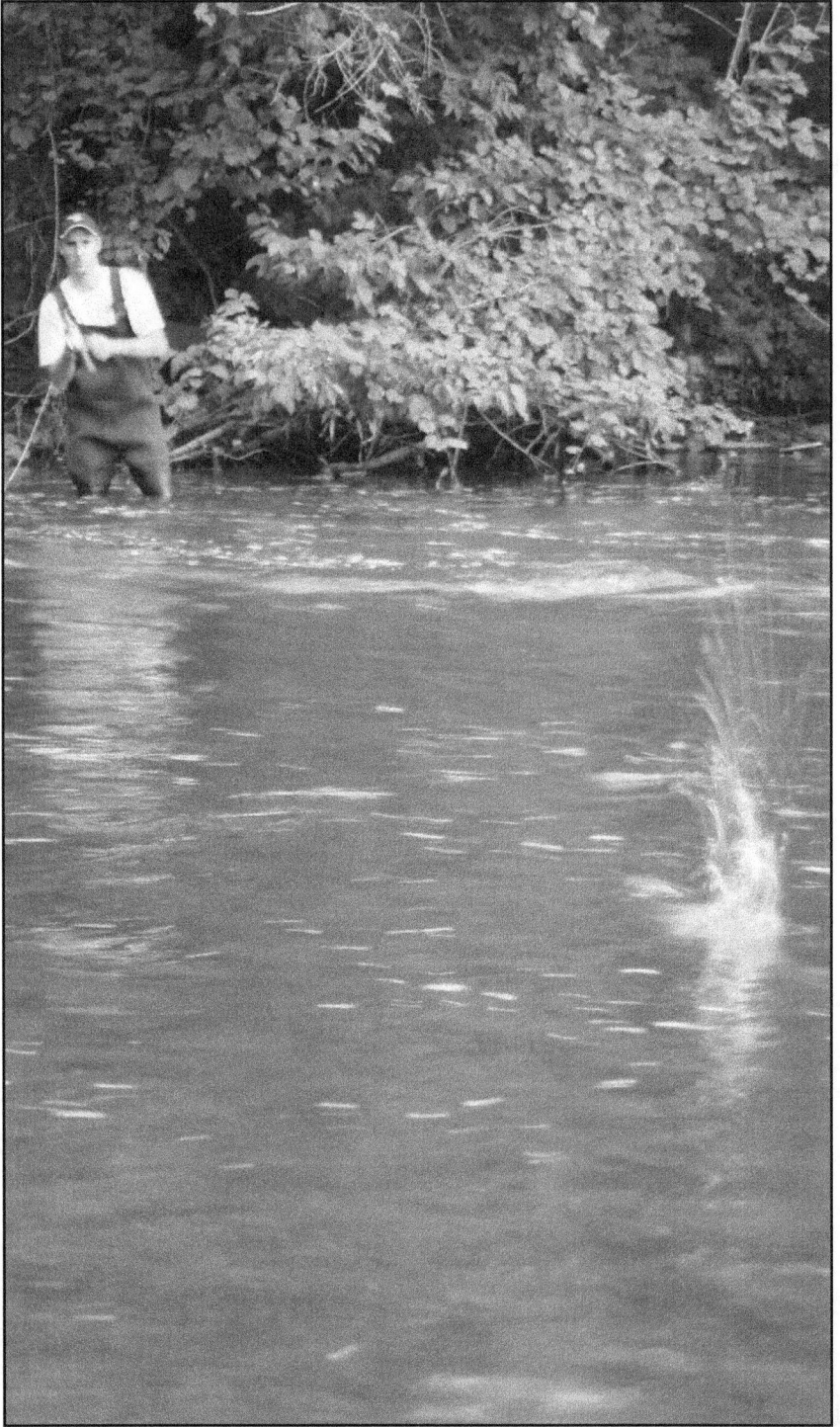

several feet off the bottom of the river. A traditional lead head jig often drops below a suspended fish and out of the strike zone. However a suspended jig places it in front of the fish. Additionally, research has shown that walleye will strike a lure above them or at the same depth as them more often than a lure below them. With this challenge in mind, floating jigs were created to present the lure higher in the water column.

The larger the floating head, the more foam used, and the higher it floats in the water column. How high really depends on the leader length and current speed. A faster current speed pushes the floating jig lower in the water. I have seen some unofficial studies that show at 1 mph a floating jig floats about one foot up from the bottom for every foot of leader line. In the turbulent waters they do not float nearly that high in the water column.

Picking the right amount of leader line seems like a monotonous detail, but leader length controls the depth and natural look of the floater. The longer the leader line, the higher the floater resides in the water column. It is common to run a 1 to 4 foot leader depending on the location of the fish. To stretch the boundaries, I have been known to occasionally push 7 foot leaders. That seems absurd, but has made the difference on a few days. I do not usually like leaders this long, because they make casting so difficult. Floating jigs are a valuable option that allows you to precisely fish at the right depth.

LEAD HEAD JIGS

There is nothing more adaptable and versatile then a lead head jig. These little nuggets of gold have produced more walleye across the United States than any other lure, and after the walleye run is over the White Bass, Smallmouth Bass and Crappies all love to gobble them up. Let's discuss a few popular models before talking about jig fishing techniques.

Jigs also come in various styles, weights, and hook sizes. Bullet heads, minnow, arrowhead, tear drop, gum-ball are a few of the most popular styles. The list goes on and on depending on your needs. Bullet heads are standard down at the river, but do not narrow your focus on that lead head. An old timer taught me that lesson the hard way during the post spawn. While targeting the final few walleye in the river he stood there pulling walleye after walleye out

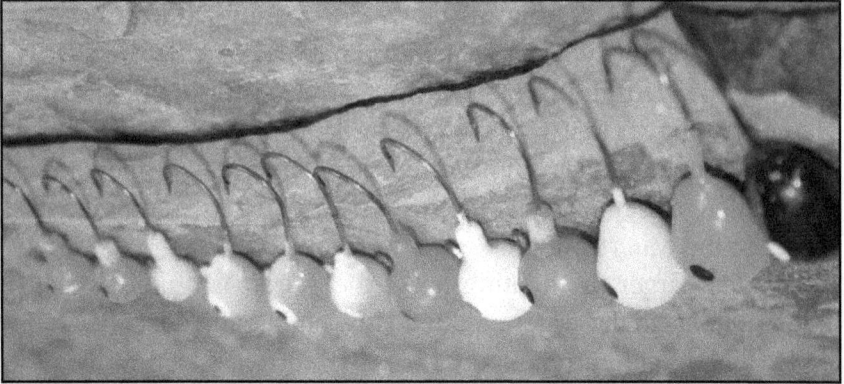

Once the jig hits the water, count the seconds until you hit bottom. Then as you cast into different locations of the river continue to count. Those locations with the longest countdown are the deepest. This will reveal hidden holes when the surface waters do not reveal the underwater secrets.

of the water while the rest of us could only catch white bass. After a bit, I wanted to unlock his secret to success. While getting some tips in the warming water he showed me his ultra-minnow lead head with halogen painted eyes. I chuckled a bit, but I am always willing to try out a new technique.

When he offered one of his jigs up, I did not hesitate – I jumped on the offer! I quickly snapped off my rig and worked to secure the ultra-minnow jig with a polymer knot. After pulling it tight I slipped on a grub and was ready for action. Just a couple casts later I felt the unmistakable nudge on my line. Pulling tight on the line there was a head shake, then the drag squealed as he ran. This was no white bass; a walleye had found his way to my jig. Upon leaving the river, I went directly to the local tackle shop to buy some ultra-minnow lead heads. Since then, I have started using various different lead head jigs with great success.

A good lead head jig starts with a quality hook. Matching the hook size to the grub is important, but I try to use the biggest hook available. Those with larger gap sizes provide a better hookup. Painted heads are ideal for finesse fishing, but during the main run in April I often use unpainted heads because so many are lost.

Although so many fishermen are using floating jigs, do not

These three different lead heads offer a very different presentation; Minnow, Fathead, and TipUp lead jig heads. They look differently when sitting on the bottom and swim differently in the river. Do not always settle for the standard round heads.

overlook lead. Lead heads are often used to work the bottom of the river, and are an ideal solution when walleye begin hugging tight to structure. This generally occurs after the water rises and heavy current prevails.

One of my favorite ways to fish is using a Carolina rig with a small lead head trailing. The river current keeps the lure bouncing but it does not drop to the bottom like a heavier head. My sliding weight further up the line enables me to cast farther and keep the lure close to the bottom. Not many try this technique, but it is very successful.

JIG DECISIONS

Whether a floating jig or lead head is used, the exact weight is important. The right weight puts the lure on the bottom and presents it at the right speed. The heavier the weight, the slower it moves downstream. The lighter the weight, the faster it moves. Too light, and there might not be any contact with the bottom. While working a hole, walleye will stack in different locations depending on the conditions. A lighter weight is needed for suspended walleye so the jig hangs or slowly falls into the hole. On days when they are hugging the bottom, a heavy weight is needed to drop right down into the hole. A few real life examples follow.

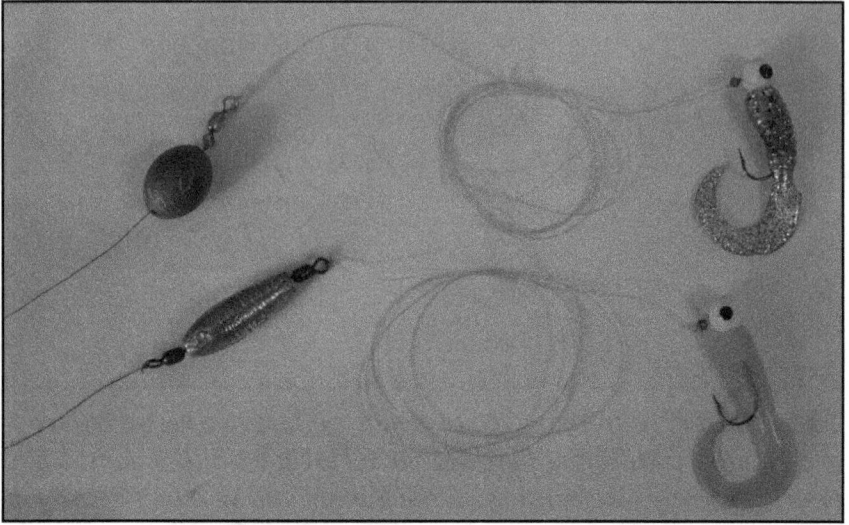

The traditional Carolina rig (top) and a modified version with an inline sinker (lower) are both shown here. Both systems are extremely effective walleye fishing setups in the Maumee River.

Here is the ideal method to catch suspended fish inside a deep hole. I like to cast just above the head of the hole. You will feel the weight bouncing along the bottom, followed by a void when you enter the hole. The void will continue until you drop to the bottom of the hole or the lure swings out of the hole. This motion of the lure through the hole allows you to catch those suspended fish inside.

If this is not working, it is time to increase lure weight. Cast again above the head of the hole, but this time you will feel the weight bouncing harder against the rocks, followed by a void. This time it will only last a couple seconds before feeling the bouncing again, this time against the bottom of the hole. This simple modification just changed the water column that you fished.

While smallmouth fishing I bounce my jig along the bottom to provide some additional movement. Here it often best to use a slow reel and keep constant tension. From the time you cast, reel up the slack line so there is tension and feeling. However, fishing walleye is about contact with the bottom. Often lures are not being presented in the strike zone. My goal is to put a lure in front of the walleye's nose on every cast. The more times the lure is set in the strike zone the better the odds are of having a walleye strike.

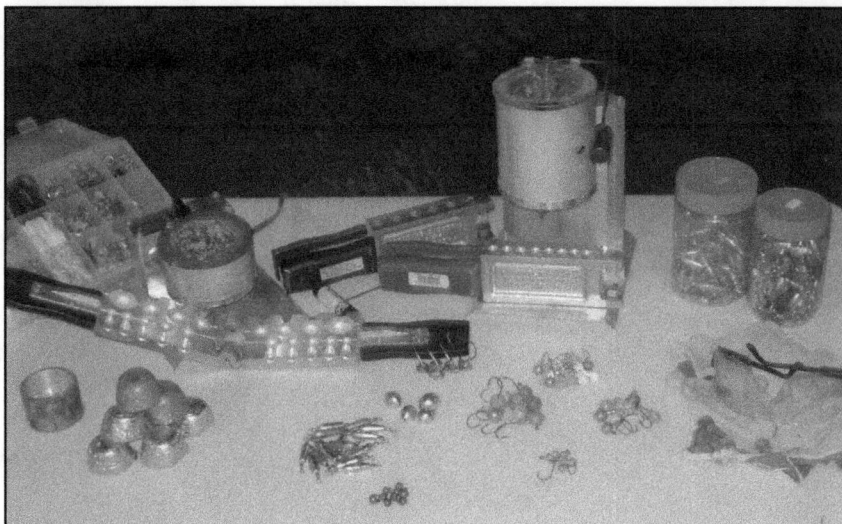

There is a table full of tools to make lead head jigs, bullet weights, inline sinkers, and many other fishing lures and sinkers.

POURING LEAD

With the economy in a slump and gas prices continuing to rise, fisherman are looking for ways to cut corners. Instead of cutting back on our love of fishing we need to get resourceful. Whether you're jigging lead heads or casting inline lures on a submerged hump, lead has often been the material of choice. Practically everyone who fishes in the rivers has a number of weights made from lead. These two methods, inline rigs and jigs, take more walleye across the state than any other method.

Walleye love to hug the bottom between large rock points, which are known for eating jigs. The turbulent current in the river routinely wedges lures into the toughest snags. While targeting walleye among the rocks, losing lures is just part of the game. Over the years I've found it fun to make my own jigs, inline sinkers, and bullet weights. It's very simple and easy to get started, and is a great way to save some money.

Any time you're dealing with molding hot metal you first need to think about safety. You only get two eyes to last your entire life. Don't be stupid; wear safety glasses. I've been pouring lures for over 25 years and found it's easier on my arms and hands to always

An invaluable tool to have in the water is a hook sharpener. Rocks dull, bend, and break off hook tips. A sharp hook will catch more walleye.

wear a long sleeve shirt and gloves. Some metal splatter is inevitable while pouring. Any water, even small amounts, will explode into steam and splatter hot lead. Hot metal sticks to your skin until it cools, which doesn't feel good.

There also is a health risk when dealing with lead, so only proceed after reading all the manufacturer's precautions. To minimize any hazard don't eat or drink while working with or after touching lead. Keep your hands away from your mouth, including smoking.

Make sure your setup is stable and your cords are out of the way or duct taped to the floor. Only work in areas with good ventilation; sufficient air flow should carry away any fumes.

The first thing you'll need is a production lead melting pot. These come in a variety of sizes and models. There are two main types on the market; those with bottom spouts and those that require a ladle to pour. Bigger is not always better a medium to small melting pot works very well. I feel the best pot for pouring lures is your bottom spout. They are easy to use and relatively fast when pouring large quantities.

Those without a bottom spout require using a ladle to pour lead. I like to use these pots to melt lead into manageable chunks. The first melt also burns off the majority of impurities from the lead.

A tackle tamer which have traditionally been used for worm harnesses can be adapted to use for pre-tied floating leaders.

The second thing you'll need is a lead mold to pour the hot metal into. Many tackle shops offer a variety of molds, from jigs to bullet weights. You'll often find molds that make a variety of sized lures. My inline sinker mold allows me to pour from ¼ oz to ¾ oz size sinkers. This allows me to buy one mold instead of 5 different one-size molds. Once you sink a few dollars into the equipment the rest is fairly inexpensive. If you compare the cost of the equipment to the cost of replacing lost lures at a bait and tackle shop, you will find that the equipment pays for itself in a few spring river fishing seasons

Now it's time to get started. Your goal is to get products as inexpensively as possible. This is where you should be thinking bulk. There are many lure making wholesalers that will sell swivels, hooks, and more for very low prices, and usually the more you buy the bigger discount you get. I've often found deep discounts at wholesale fishing stores or online. There are many bait shops and online stores that are always competing for your business.

Lead can be purchased from any metal dealer or scrap yard. Use caution here and only purchase clean lead. Although you might be able to purchase a bucket full of dirty car wheel weights, I don't advise you to go this route, no matter how cheap wheel weights are. They cause havoc on your melting pots. The excess impurities will gunk up bottom spout melting pots and the excessive oil burning off will cause heavy amounts of smoke. Even with clean lead you will have some garbage burning off. This is why I use two pots: one to make small one pound clean lead chunks and another I only use with clean lead to pour jigs and weights. Many who pour lures have found this is a valuable method.

As a dedicated walleye fisherman I also know many other walleye enthusiasts, and we all lose plenty of jigs. Rather than purchasing replacements from a shop, many of us find that making our

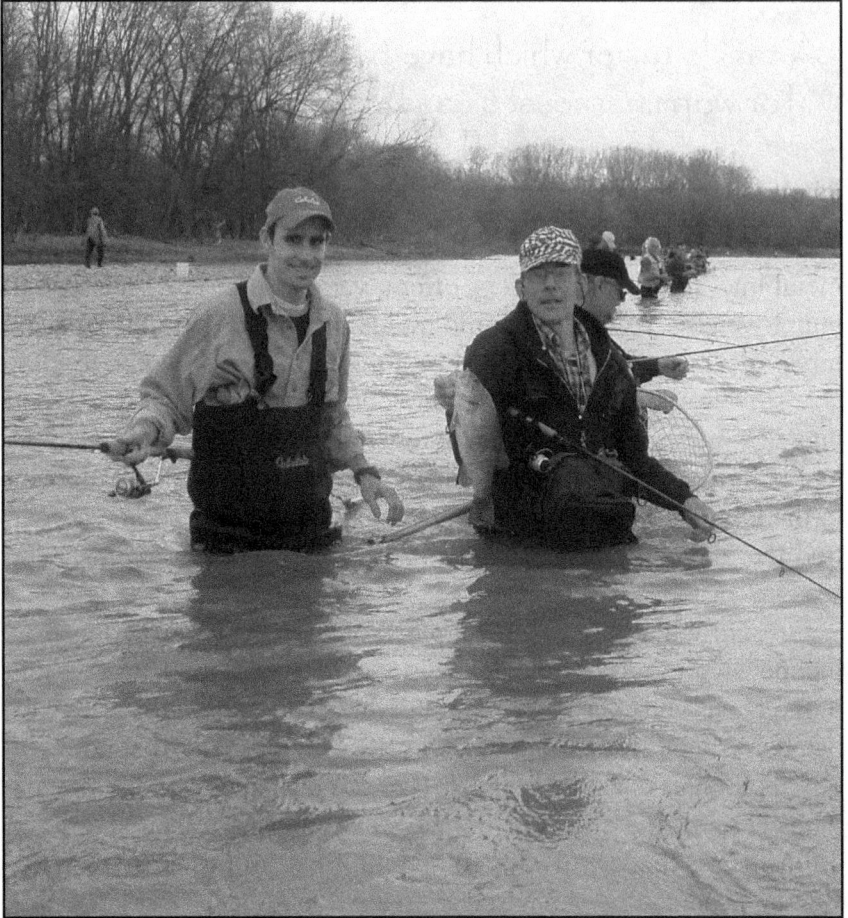

My father caught this nice smallmouth bass while using a home-made jig. The Maumee River provides surprise fish like this one between the walleye madness.

own jigs is more affordable. Initially, the cost of the pot and molds might cause you to hesitate, but after losing a few dozen jigs you will easily make your money back. Pouring lead is also something that can be done during the off-season and shared among friends, extending the savings to others as well.

Making jigs is not just for walleye; these lures are used to catch everything from bluegills to pike. The options are endless once you start; jig molds, sinker molds, and other specialty molds are readily available. Take a look at your tackle box and you will see that the options are unlimited.

Several years ago I was fishing near an older gentleman who seemed to be standing on a lucky rock. His casts were perfect and he was landing fish after fish. I politely asked him what his secret was and he handed me a small minnow lead jig head. I was a bit skeptical at first but several casts later I was a believer. He poured his own heads; this one was a "Do-It Ultra Minnow Head Jig." The way his lure cut the water made it fall perfectly into the strike zone.

Building your lures allows you to make custom adjustments and add to your mold collection. My collection of molds has grown from one into nearly a dozen. As I find a need I continue to add molds for standard jigs, inline weights, minnow jig, or bullet jig molds.

I am a firm believer that choosing the lure color can make all the difference. The right color combination can cause the fish to start biting like mad. Do not get stuck thinking your jig heads will just be silver; adding color is easy. Several companies make paint to dip heads into. I've also used powder paint, which makes multicolored heads easy. Some paints even contain additives that reflect UV light, allowing a fish to see it farther away. Each type of paint requires different procedures to get the best adhesion, so please read the manufacturer's instructions before beginning the process.

Once you start adding pizzazz you can be as creative as you want, adding eyes, faded colors, or anything else you can imagine. For the river, I keep it simple because I lose so many to the rocks!

Knowing I made the lures that ultimately aided in catching the fish gives me great pride. Each summer I spend a few hours pouring lead for myself. It's a good feeling to know I can make three-dozen bullet weights for under a dollar. If you're tired of buying jigs to replace the ones you've lost to the rocks, try pouring your own. I know a few fishermen that have caught the fever for making lures. For them, this has turned into a second hobby by branching out into making many different kinds of lures. I simply enjoy sticking to the basics and make just enough for family and a few close friends to use each year. It's very inexpensive and in short order you'll have a pile of lures ready to tackle the spring walleye.

Chapter 9

It's More Than a Feeling

Figuring out the right lure weight, size and color does not guarantee walleye success. I spent many of my earlier years struggling with this aspect until realizing one important fact: If you can't feel or don't know what a walleye bite feels like you'll spend hours using the right technique and walk away empty handed.

This is a major stumbling block for many fishermen regardless of their experience level. When I was younger I stood next to my older brother who would land five times as many fish as I did. He would tell me exactly what he was doing, where the fish were laying, yet I still didn't get it. It wasn't until much later when I really started paying attention that I starting filling the gap between my brother and I. I still remember the first day that I out fished him. After nearly ten years of chasing his shadow that was the beginning of a whole new fishing era.

Walleye can be some of the most finicky fish. Combine this with tough river conditions and it's amazing we catch them at all. When fishing a Carolina rig in turbulent waters it's very hard to tell what is a bite or a rock. I'm going to discuss how you can quadruple your hook up through a few refined techniques.

Understanding what is under the surface of the water goes a long way. Since you can't see through the murky waters you need to feel through your fishing rod what is happening under the water. Those fishermen that can feel every rock and stick on the bottom are often the best fishermen. It is just like looking at a topographical map, but some of the river bottom features change from year to year. Heavy ice jams and high water moves rocks making changes enough to cause places to go hot and cold from year to year. Being able to tell the difference between fish, a rock, or leftover fishing line gives you eyes below the surface of the water. And with some practice you'll be able to tell when your lure falls off the edge into a hole.

It's pretty funny; if you cast over and over in the same spot you'll begin to notice the terrain under the water. You will feel the same rock and even tangled fishing line on the bottom of the river. With this knowledge you can begin to understand how the walleye are using the murky terrain.

Fishing lines feels like a drag, the lure stops bouncing and slides bouncing very slightly. Even the littlest things, like a leaf on the end of your lure has a very different feeling. You wouldn't imagine a little tiny leaf would make it feel completely different. Everything on the river floor offers a different feeling.

So many anglers are waiting for a walleye to take off like a largemouth bass exploding on a topwater lure, like a tug-of-war game. I think this is where most people fail. A better angler waits until they see slack or a lift in their rod. This means a walleye picked up their lure. Most bites are so subtle it's a lift not a tug. The best way I find to notice these subtle differences is by using a high quality, fast action rod combined with braided line. This combination gives me the ability to feel every rock I bounce against.

Understanding how walleye eat allows you to understand what you want to feel. Many times walleye open up their mouth and suck in the bait. While using a Carolina rig you will just barely feel him pick up the lure. What happens is they will actually pick up on your lure ever so gracefully. So instead of your lure continuing to bounce along you'll stop feeling the lure bounce on the bottom. That is what the feeling is all about. When there is not that bounce any more that is when you need to set the hook.

The greatest tip I can give you is to watch your rod tip. Look

Windy days make for tough conditions. Not because the fish don't bite but because the fishermen cannot feel the bite.

for your lure to stop. Also if you are having a hard time feeling the action put your index finger on the line. This takes away the middle man. You are feeling what is happening on the line which is the piece of equipment that is connecting you to the fish.

While fishing with a close friend I noticed the amount of slack in her line. Cast after cast she left her bail open for a few seconds then after closing the bail she let the current pull the line tight; which took a considerable amount of time. In this location most of the fish being caught were directly out in front of us. Because there was too much slack in her line she was not feeling any of the bites. Before she had a chance to set the hook the fish had already spit out the lure. A short while later we discussed where the walleye were

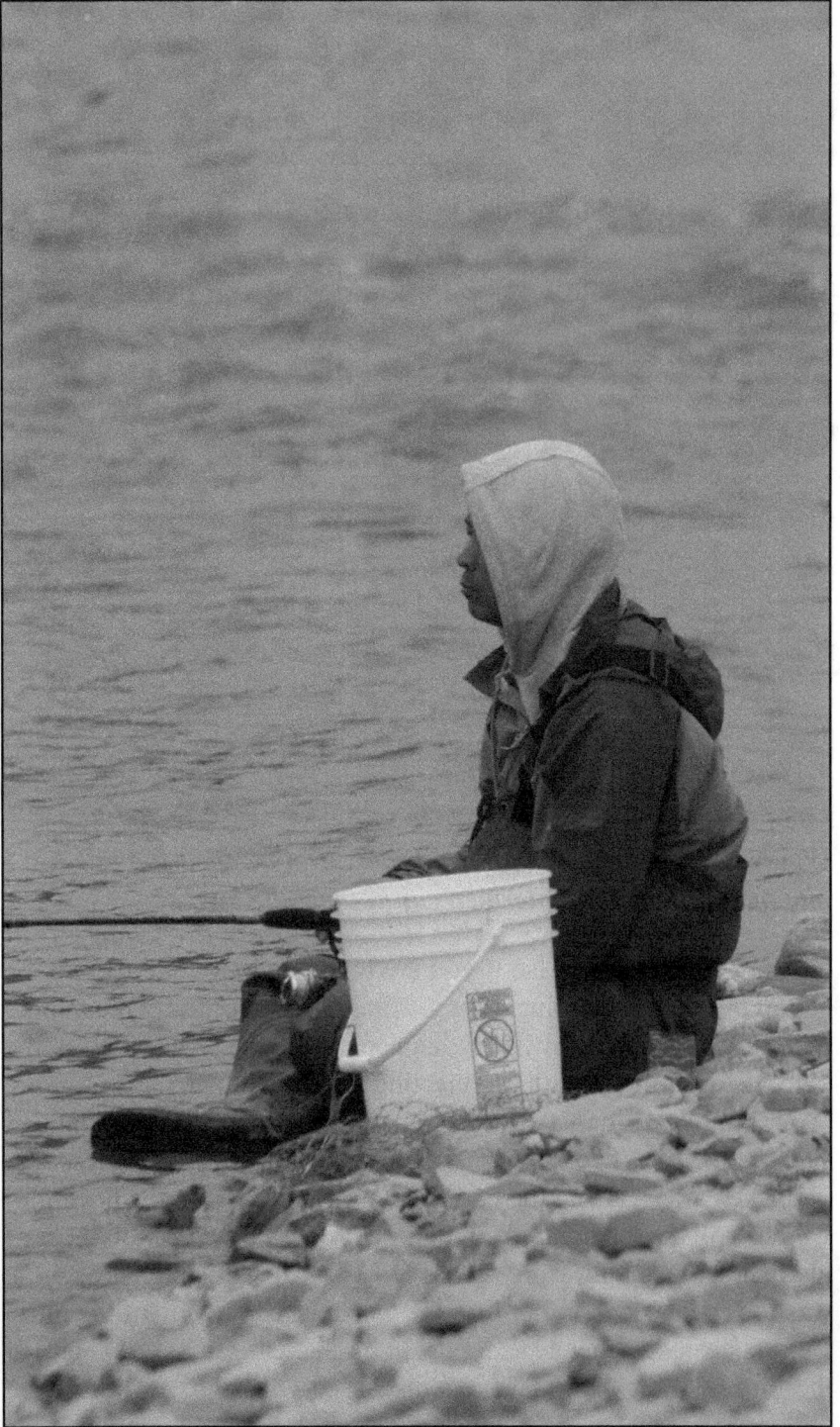

located and how to increase her odds. This slight modification in attention helped her to start catching walleye like many others around her. After casting it is best to reel in any extra slack in the fishing line. Slack in the line does not allow you to feel the fish or bottom of the river. A tight line aids in feeling so you can feel every little rock, soft spot, or walleye. This helps me put eyes down on the river floor from the second my lure hits the water until it is back in my hand.

HOW WIND AFFECTS RIVER FISHING

Becoming an expert angler comes by mastering every technique in every water and weather condition. And topping the charts for toughest conditions are cold windy days. Even aggressive fish can be tough during adverse weather. High winds dramatically reduce sensitivity because your line above the water is blowing slack bends in your line. This slack causes you to lose a great deal of feeling.

Not only does it wreak havoc on feeling fish but it plays tricks on being able to put your lure in the strike zone. The Maumee River is a tributary to Lake Erie, a great lake that is affected immensely by east and west winds. Northern or easterly winds will rock the water in Lake Erie towards Toledo. Heavy winds in this direction will push water back up stream in the Maumee River. Even though the water is running downstream towards Lake Erie, the current slows down and water is actually pushing back into the river. Below the last set of rapids the water level will rise with a heavy wind blowing back upstream. This is caused because the normal water level of the lake has increased. This is very similar to how a high tide works.

What I have noticed is the fishing locations on the bottom half of Bluegrass Island and extending towards Lake Erie (downstream) get hit the hardest with heavy north and east winds. The water slows and tougher conditions pursue. But the northern portion of Bluegrass Island and farther upstream does not get affected as harshly. The east end of Bluegrass Island offers the first set of rapids. I believe this reduces the leaning bowl effect from Lake Erie. Don't get me wrong, windy conditions affect every area, it just hits anything downstream from the rapids the hardest.

While fishing these conditions, it is a time to really pay attention to how the lure floats downstream. Finding the exact right

The direction and speed of the wind help me determine which location to fish. This day we selected the right location even with winds gusting over 30 miles per hour.

weight to move the lure past the walleye is critical. Select a lure that is too heavy and it will just sit on the bottom. Too light of a weight and the lure will float above and too quickly through the strike zone. In many cases I start out casting a heavier lure and then lighten up from there.

On the contrary, winds blowing from the west or southwest cause the river current to pick up speed. Even during low water conditions the current becomes very strong as water is pushed out of the river. This also causes the water levels to fall much quicker than without the wind. The long stretch from south of Waterville down to the 475 bridge is that largest effected region. High wind pushes very

It sounds simple but feeling when a walleye bites your jig will drastically increase your success. This can be a difficult task in the river currents.

hard and has time to build up speed.

In most cases fishing during high winds is a time to go with heavier weights. A heavier lead weight helps with casting and slows down the presentation. The number one reason for not catching walleye in windy conditions is the lack of feeling the bite. When the wind dies down is when you can feel the bite and therefore catch more fish. It has nothing to do with whether or not they were biting while the wind was blowing hard.

Getting yourself tucked into a location that is not affected will help you gain feeling. Look at the wind direction and search out locations on the river where it bends around protecting you from the wind. This will give you protection, making it a more comfortable day on the water. And even if the fishing is slower, you will be able to feel the bites you're getting. And with higher winds pushing and pulling on the river currents, places that traditionally produce sometimes go flat while other protected structures turns on.

I have a spot right near the shore that turns on during high winds. The rock point has a deep drop off that most anglers walk through this hole to reach deeper pools in the middle of the river. Walleye stack behind the rock point to protect themselves from the strong currents when the wind picks up. Understanding this phenomenon can help anglers pick out other places along the river that could be holding hungry walleye.

After spending millions of hours in the past 25 years in the Maumee River I know that walleye can be some of the most finicky eaters. Understanding the way they eat and getting in tune with what a walleye feels like are some of the most important aspects of catching more fish. Understand what's going on below the murky water without actually visually seeing it. You're going to need to perfect visualizing river structure through feeling the bounces of your rod.

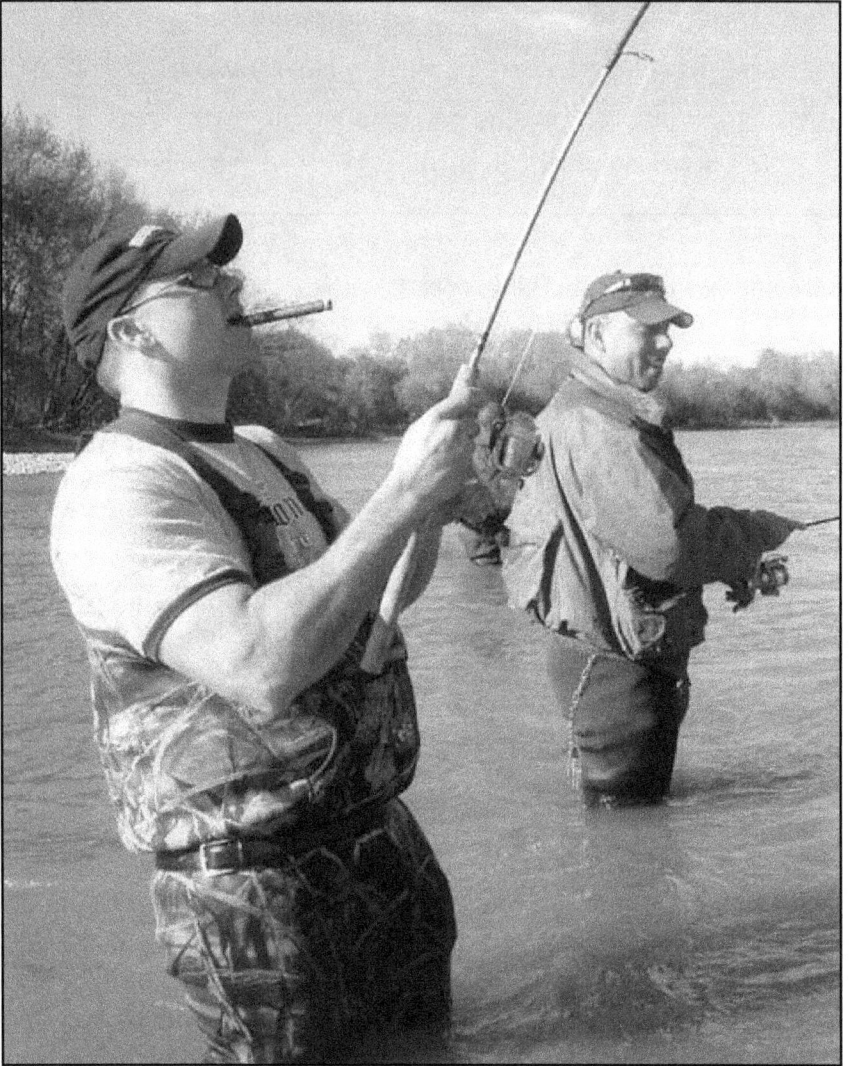

Watching the tip of your rod is another way to ensure walleye are not escaping before you notice the bite.

It doesn't matter if you're using the prefect strategy in the right location at the right time. If you don't feel the walleye biting your line than your success will be very poor. Fine tune your techniques of feeling the bite of a walleye and even an average fisherman will go home with many fish.

TIPS FOR FEELING MORE

Nothing much feels like the real thing. A solid Tap, Tap, on the rod and then a hard pull of a walleye. It is a wonderful sensation to have an aggressive fish completely tackle the jig. So often this is not the case. I can tell you from personal experience that feeling a walleye bite is a fundamental skill which separates those incredible fishermen from those who are just good. I have spent more years while growing up in my brother's shadow trying to catch up. He always had more and bigger fish then I had on the stringer. The year I finally began using a quality fishing rod and began to understand the "feel" was when I first out fished him.

Understanding your equipment helps a fisherman become better. In the spring, my fishing rod is an extension of my arm. I become so entrenched in fishing I can feel just about everything that touches the other end of my jig.

So how do you become better at knowing when a fish has taken your lure? The best way to describe it is the void of rock. If anything feels different then set the hook. If it feels stuck then set the hook. I know that many of you are concerned about sinking a hook deeper into those unforgiving rocks. If this is a concern then simply pick up and feel the pressure then set the hook. If a walleye is felt then immediately set the hook! Walleye have soft mouths, bring it tight and reel. Do not let your bass fishing instincts kick in or you will rip it from the walleyes lips.

So any time you lose the feeling of the bounce or vibration then there is a great chance of a walleye. Lastly if the line goes slack then pull it tight. Initially there will be many times a hook is set without a walleye on the end. After attempting many hook sets this will become more instinctual once you have gained the "feel" of the walleye.

SUCCESSFUL LANDING

Landing walleye can be tricky business. There are so many things that must go right to land a walleye, such as dealing with heavy current, navigating sharp rocks, and fishermen in close proximity. All of these items are a recipe for disaster. Through all of this dismay the right approach will help you land more walleye successfully.

Walleye have soft mouths and jigs can easily be pulled out

if pulling hard on the rod. A solid hook set is necessary but don't go overboard. Often with a good hook set the walleye will fight out of the deeper water then eventually surface with his mouth open. At this time I work to keep him sliding over the surface to keep constant pressure on the line until he slides into my hands. Working together with those around you is important. When walleye are being landed by the fishermen near you, pause before casting again. Let the fisherman next to you bring his catch partway in before casting. Do not cast on top of his line, this causes mayhem for both parties. Working the water around you comes into play while fishing a crowd. When I have a fish on I will take one step out so I am slightly in front of the crowd. This allows my fish to slide past others without problems. Additionally when others have fish around me I take a step backwards. This allows them to retrieve a fish without tangling in my gear. Walleye have a mind of their own and a last minute run could end up tangled around your legs.

Netting fish with long leaders takes some careful navigating. First, know your leader length. Once you see the leader line it indicates how close the fish is. Also you only get one chance to net the fish right before he will make a dash to the side, be ready. Once I see the leader is close to the tip I pull my rod hand high. Bring the rod tip up and back to close the distance while the walleye swims in front of you. At the same time scoop him from behind. Once he is in the net I'll slowly bring the rod arm down letting the fish fall into the net. This is a true tested technique that works. Scooping a walleye from the side allows for a greater chance of knocking him off or flipping out. This is especially important on bigger walleye that do not fit well into a river net.

When my fish come into the landing, I work hard to keep them in the water. I do this because fish in water stay calm. Picking them up causes the walleye to flop around and get off. Even after netting the fish I keep him in the water until he is on the stringer. Keep the net under him until he is on the stringer. Out of the net he is only one flop away from freedom.

The critical time is the last three feet; this is when more people lose fish. This is caused because the walleye is fighting hard, the walleye becomes spooked, or we are scrambling for a net. To be

Netting a walleye from the tail forward will allow them to fall deep into the net.

ready to land a walleye successfully means thinking about landing one beforehand. It sounds simple, but have the stringer clips ready and the net strapped to your wader belt and accessible within reach. Right when I get a bite and the walleye is still far out in the river it is time to prepare. Remove the gloves, pull around the net, and be ready. When the walleye hits the final stretch you should already be mentally prepared to land him. In close, the current can slow down. Any loss of pressure on the hook is detrimental. Keep a steady pull and don't bounce the rod.

If landing fish with a net becomes easy then it is time to begin landing fish by hand. On some of my first trips to the Maumee my older brother made me land all my fish without a net. This was a hard lesson but learning to catch walleye without a net really helped me handle fish. It takes a steady hand and a death grip to be successful. In those early years I lost many fish. Although landing walleye by hand may not be for you, it can be fun or maddening. That depends on the success.

Landing walleye by hand is much easier if the conditions are right. When there is some current and the water is close to the fishermen's waist it is advantageous. So many people ask me how it's done. When the fish rises to the top keep constant pressure all the way in. Bouncing or loss of pressure on the fish will be a sure fire way to lose him. When you are pulling the walleye up there is only one opportunity to land him cleanly. Keep him close, pull the rod hand high but push him against the front of the waders while grabbing his head hard. Whether you push him against your leg or between your legs, both work great. Keep the fish downstream and grab him in one motion. Once the fish begin swimming around tension is lost and so is your fish. The walleye will still be energetic and anything done to scare him will cause another run that will likely end up in a lost fish. When I have a hard time seeing the fish I will run my hand down the fishing line until I can grab his head. Once you have him make sure to bring the stringer right over to hook him up. I keep the fish on the top or in the water simply to keep him calm. Moving a fish around before he is on the stringer causes many lost fish.

There are two techniques I use depending on the amount of people fishing. On normal days I work in the walleye gently until I have them in close. When the crowd is extremely heavy I work hard to bring the fish out of the deep holes and pull them in fast. This keeps others from tangling into my fish. There is no question I lose far more fish using this technique, up to 25% more. On busy days those fish can be lost in tangles or from others mistakes. Again I only do this when I am having difficulty with novice fishermen near me.

Walleye are finicky fish. Improve your ability to feel the bite of a walleye and you will drastically improve your daily catch. This becomes most important on windy days. The right location will help improve your catch. Lastly, when the bite is tough every fish caught is important. Work hard to ensure each one is landed with perfection. Doing all these things right helps you go home with many more fish.

Chapter 10

Double or Nothing

Most discussions around walleye strategies revolve around lure presentation, water depth, weather conditions, barometric pressure, etc. But here, I am going to talk about stacking the odds in your favor regardless of the conditions, lure or water temperature. After years of fishing I have come to realize that it is all the little things which make all the difference. Primarily finding an exact pattern and sticking with it throughout the fishing trip. This is exactly what the professional walleye anglers we watch on TV due to an extreme degree. Once you figure out a pattern you need to do it over and over again. You really need to pay attention to what you are doing and when the fish are biting. Then once a patterns evolves do it over and over again.

With a walleye pattern it is necessary to figure it out rather quickly. With low creel limits a patterns needs to be identified on your first bite and solidified as you catch more. Whether you catch that fish or just get a bit remember everything about the situation. If you do not even know how far you casted your chances of repeating are slim. Buy a lottery ticket instead.

Several years ago I was guiding a couple of fishermen into a spot I had not fished in several years. Within a couple cast, I had a fish on the line. It was a nice size male walleye, perfect for the

***Working together as a team we found a presentation that worked
and caught a couple limits of walleye in short order.***

frying pan. Within minutes I switched everyone I was guiding to
the exact rig and had them casting to the exact location the first
fish was picked up. Within thirty minutes every fisherman had their
daily limit of walleye. Those fishermen around us were amazed,
calling us lucky. But it wasn't luck it was the fact that we were very
strategic in placing the lure in front of the walleye more times than
anyone else around.

      Every time you catch a fish ask yourself several questions.
Why was the fish there, what was he doing, what was the depth,
what was your lure presentation, and was he near any underwater
structure? What where you doing that caused them to bite? Walleye
run in schools so if you can repeat your action your chances are im-
mense of getting another immediate hookup. Was it a long or short
cast, 3/4 oz or 5/8 oz inline sinker, pink head with white grub, 3 or 6
foot leader, etc.? All of these questions are critical to your success.

Anyone who has fished the Maumee River for very long can tell you there are a few remarkable days each year. When everything is right make the most of it by fishing as many consecutive days as possible.

Other patterns to pay attention to are the weather and water conditions. Did the sun begin to shine before the bite turned on or did the wind die down. These are all factors that will have effects on when the marble eyes begin biting. All of these factors are subtle differences but these types of details pay big dividends.

What it really comes down to is, doing 25 different things right every time. When you do this all right you will out fish just about every other person on the river. As fisherman we have the ability to pay attention and decipher the pattern. Figuring out the pattern that others could not makes me better at successfully catching fish which gives me great pride.

It amazes me the difference an eighth of an ounce or even line diameter. Each person is carrying different types of equipment. Even if you match weight, lure color, and size it might not work exactly the same as the next person. If one person is running low drag braded line and the other monofilament they may be offering different presentations. If your neighbor is catching fish and you are not, absolutely try to match their setup. It may be one or a number of things they are doing. Try this then play around with your weight. Remember an extra foot of leader line on your Carolina rig can make the difference an empty or full stringer of walleye.

Stacking the odds is about doing everything right over and over again. What works for you may not work for someone else. But pay attention to those details and learn from other successful fishermen. They are doing something different and often have years of experience in the river.

WHEN THE FISHING IS GOOD

Looking back at the past years fishing logs and one important fact sticks out. Although there are thousands of walleye that migrate into the river each spring there are only a number of phenomenal days each year. If you miss those red hot days it could take you the rest of the season to catch up.

I can remember when a warming trend came through in mid-March. There were record high days causing the water to warm quicker than normal. These warmer water temperatures cause a huge influx of walleye to push upstream earlier than predicted. On my end work obligations kept me away from the river. I kept telling myself that it could not be that good, it was not time yet. Finally I saw a break in my schedule towards the end of the week. My plans were to leave work early to experience this early run of fish. Unfortunately the day before I was expected to fish the temperature snapped cold and the snow began to fly. This cold weather dropped the water temperature over five degrees and halted the early run. This cold front held a tight grip on Northern Ohio for the next two weeks.

I have seen this happen time and time again. I knew better then to hold off fishing but that circumstance reiterated those facts back into my head again. Going forward I fish when the fishing is excellent because there are relatively few days when it is red hot.

TOUGH MENTAL EDGE

Several years ago I stood next to my friend Tim who was catching fish after fish. His confidence was souring as he brought in fish after fish. It didn't take me long to match his exact setup; lure color, weight, leader length and more. He quickly pointed out where the fish were coming from and how they hit. Knowing that I introduced him to the river, I knew I could outfish him. I concentrated on what he was doing and stepped closer and closer to him. I still couldn't get into the groove and began to get frustrated.

After a bit he noticed my frustration and offer to swap spots, which had to work. I jumped at the opportunity and slide right onto his lucky rock. This had to be the trick. The drift must have been just right where he was standing. To my dismay he continued to catch more fish as I was distracted by his success. Now that was terrible, my unlucky rock was pulling out fish. Soon we decided to move to another part of the river. I needed a change in scenery and a fresh section of water to fish.

Having the confidence to stick it out during tough fishing conditions is very rewarding. A 27 inch walleye was the reward for adapting to a new technique when the bite was slow.

Soon we hit a brand new section of the river and we stood next to each other again. With Tim's confidence souring het immediately got into fish. Slightly disgruntled I pulled up and moved downstream, I couldn't handle it any longer. In little time my attitude got better, I started focusing on myself and I began catching walleye. And I really starting getting walleye from places I hadn't touch fish earlier.

Some of the best professional walleye anglers have a tough mental attitude. Even when fishing is down they keep their wits

Confidence builds upon itself! When things are going right continue to build upon your skills to help when conditions get tough.

with themselves. This mental and emotion control is something that keeps your head in the game. They are brimming with confidence and let that flow into their fishing. It's simply amazing because these types of people can sell ice to an Eskimo.

Fishing with confidence sounds simple but it is something that many struggle with. When you are confident in yourself, you feel knowledgeable, and are in sync with your angling skills. But even the walleye fisherman can become scattered or flustered when nothing is going right.

The first step to confidence is having a solid grasp of your angling ability. You don't understand why walleye bite or river structure you will not be confident in yourself. It is very important that when you don't understand something you pause and figure out why. Asking some of the better fisherman or local professionals will help you in the next situation. Don't just figure those conditions will not happen again.

Being able to adjust quickly to changing conditions also helps your confidence. This concept is easier said than done though. Being in a slump while others are catching walleye can crack even the most confident and knowledgeable angler. This can be handled easily by remembering this is supposed to be a fun sport. Forget about the problems, slow down, and concentrate on your own fishing ability. Take a step back and stay on task. Address what you know and adapt to what has worked in the past. Remember to keep your cool and work through your own lack of confidence.

After dealing with similar situations, it has helped me greatly to log my notes in a fishing journal so I can reference later what worked or didn't. Each situation is different; sometimes you'll get pelted with weather and water conditions.

Controlling your mental confidence adds to the ability to think on your feet making the right decisions. Many athletes consider this a tough mental edge. The higher your confidence the better you perform. When you're in control, it is easier to handle any situation you run into. Keeping yourself comfortable and maintain a resilient confidence level it allows you to stay calm.

All of these factors come together and help you stay confident. So what does all this have to do with fishing? Maintaining a strong mental attitude, staying positive under all conditions will help you feel confident. And when you feel confident you make good decisions, feel more fish bites, and catch more fish. When you feel confident, you fish with confidence.

Fishing is an individual sport. You get what you put into it. And different anglers have different goals. Some people are out to reunite with friends, others enjoy gods beautiful outdoors, and others are out to catch a fish dinner. Whatever turns you onto the river is your goal. Capturing the essence of the moment is what gets groves fisherman flocking to the banks.

Chapter 11

River Water Levels

Each spring brings fluctuating water levels that can range from flood to drought-like conditions. Given the choice, I love water that is constant and unchanged, especially if the water level is normal for the river. Fishermen are spread over the entire river and walleye push into their traditional hot spots. There seems to be more room between fishermen, giving them the space to work in their catch. However, even a slight drop in water level can change the current and move the fish. Water level is a critical aspect of river fishing.

So what do fish do under different river water conditions? When the water is rising, fish scatter out of traditional walleye structure. The flow of the river becomes too intense, forcing them to search for new locations. Small rock eddies are soon engulfed in fast flowing water. This is a tough period to fish because the walleye are moving into different locations. Once the water reaches its peak, walleye are settling into current breaks behind islands and along the shoreline. Riprap banks, brushy shorelines, and backwaters hold the majority of the walleye at these times. Then, as the water regresses back to a normal level, walleye begin moving back towards structure in the center of the river. Walleye move off the shorelines and back into deep pools, rocky structures, or other locations near the main stream. As the water continues to drop to a low level stage, walleye will concentrate in the deepest holes and best structure. They will often become very concentrated in those locations.

Fishing can be an exact science with lower water, all about placing a jig in the exact right location because the fish are so concentrated. That said, low water fishing is not without its challenges. One of the struggles faced during low water stems from fishermen having access to the entire river. With fish becoming concentrated in one area, fishermen from both sides of the river are working the same locations. Fishermen cross lines, causing tangled lines. If the water goes unchanged for an extended time, fishing becomes very predictable. Predictability is nice, but it leads to some very crowded locations.

Fluctuating water disperses people and fish into new locations. Adjusting to this slight change in water level is difficult unless a fisherman has proven locations available. Water level changes are an exciting and challenging part of river fishing.

Spring is one of my favorite times to chase river walleye. The patterns are predictable, and warming waters cause the bite to turn on. Just the same, the springtime brings rain, and lots of it. The river becomes unruly and is stained to a muddy mess. While tempting in these conditions, waiting for lower water conditions often proves to be a costly mistake. The higher waters can bring on some amazing walleye fishing.

With water conditions always changing, spring fishing can be anything but normal. One day is spent fishing the river's main channel, tossing lures into deep clear pockets of pristine water. Then a day later, after some heavy rain, those same locations are untouchable due to the high water. The gushing flow of the current terrorize the river by ripping trees out and cutting away at the shoreline. All of this disarray brings on new challenges for the river fishermen.

Each spring I become consumed by watching the weather. Looking ahead and predicting water and weather conditions becomes a compelling hobby. Watching the weather forecast along the entire river, not just the Maumee/Perrysburg, Ohio stretch, is very important.

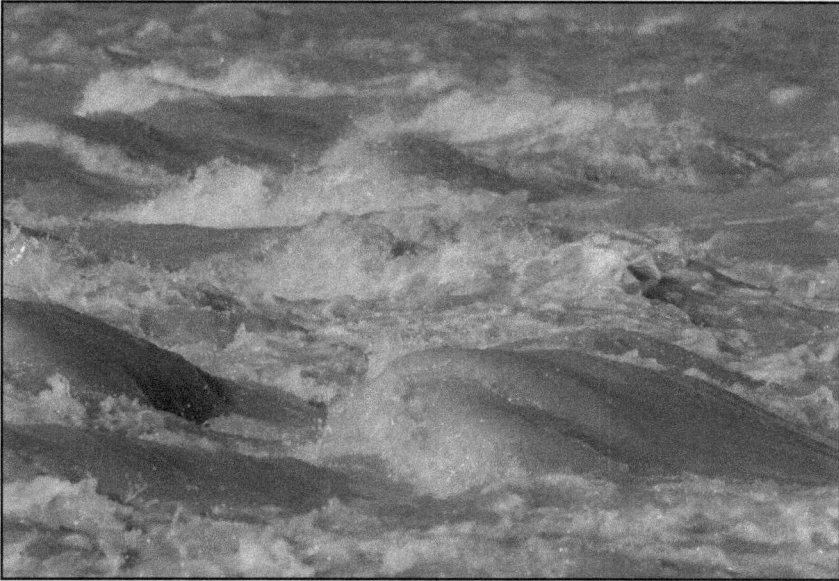

Rapids which provide excellent fishing under normal water conditions become hazardous during high water. This is a dangerous time to be in the water, fishermen should proceed with caution.

Looking over a map of the watershed for northeastern Indiana and northwestern Ohio quickly reveals the massive amount of tributaries that feed into the Maumee River. The Maumee River is formed in Fort Wayne, Indiana where the St. Joseph and St. Mary's Rivers converge. About 85 percent of the total river basin, 8,316 square miles, is agricultural. The rich farmland sheds its water into the Maumee River. This information has helped me understand how rainfall within this region affects the Maumee River water levels.

The spring weather tends to travel east across all the tributaries upstream from Maumee, Ohio. In Maumee alone, the average spring precipitation is 3.24 inches. Take into account all the run-off of rainwater into the tributaries that eventually funnel into the Maumee River and you can begin to understand how little rainfall is needed to drastically raise the river height. Any rain in this region often causes the lower portion of the Maumee River to be affected by rising flood waters, so watching the forecast extends far beyond the Maumee/Perrysburg area.

The sea level markers on the 475 Bridge are a visual indicator of water level that is used by local fishermen and Metropark officials.

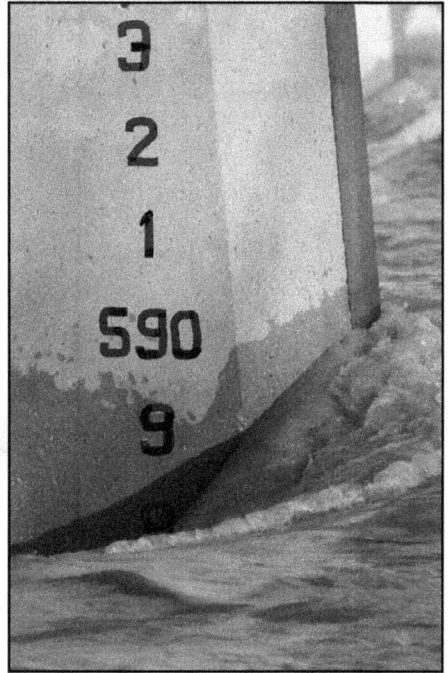

There are many scientists studying this river every day, and I have found using their expertise is by far the best method around. The U.S. Geological Survey (USGS) provides some amazing information on real-time and forecasted water levels. Every hour, the USGS reports water levels at many different points along the river. This information is then used to forecast the river's water level and when the river will rise or fall. Reading and understanding the USGS data can be challenging because it is not converted to feet above sea level. These water level markers are known by the local fisherman, used to close Metropark access, and used for local fishing reports. All of these people look to the visual sea level markings on the 475 bridge right in the middle of the prime walleye spawning grounds.

Nothing gets me more excited than high water. This turmoil initially scatters both fish and fishermen. Normal structure is flooded, leaving many fishermen guessing where to fish or watching television at home. High water fishing is very different than fishing walleye under normal water conditions. River structure and the speed of the current play a huge role in success. Too much heavy current washes the fish out of the main channel. When this happens, fishing the backwaters produces great opportunities. Any channels that offer a break from the current and slightly warmer water provide the best opportunities. But hitting the backwaters doesn't mean you want to target muddy calm pools like largemouth bass fishermen. Walleye will stick to areas with current, and as the banks are engulfed by the river, walleye begin to hang back in the brushy shoreline.

A couple years ago, I was closely tracking the higher water conditions. Several hours after the river crested, I saw the water hit a perfect level. Additionally, all the fishing reports indicated the muddy water was causing an extremely slow bite. But years of experience have taught me there are always active fish somewhere in the river system, and catching them is just a matter of putting together a presentation for those conditions. I didn't pound the brush line very long before I got my first strike. That afternoon, I was fortunate enough to fill a stringer full of walleyes in fewer than thirty minutes on a day that most would have considered a wash.

Jigging walleye along the brush is tough business. Under these conditions, the current break runs right next to the brushy island. Even when you get a hookup, the fighting walleye often gets tangled in the brush. This is when it is easy to pull a hook out of its soft mouth. Keeping the walleye clear of the shoreline requires some fancy rod work.

It was a profound moment the first time I pulled a walleye out of the water on a tube. I was smallmouth fishing a heavy current break below a dam. This got me thinking about high water walleye. Smallmouth fishermen have been using tubes for years but they often don't work their way into the walleye circuit. The Maumee River is known for floating jigs and bright grub tails. Breaking away from traditional walleye gear will help fishermen fight the tougher conditions. Tubes are great for ripping through the brushy shorelines of the river banks where high water walleye can be found.

Eddies, current break, submerged rock piles, deep holes, and even ditch channels are next on the hit list after the brushy banks. Finding these locations starts with some pre-high water legwork. High rock piles, pillars, and other structures are above water during normal water levels. These are some of the easiest structures to figure out because you can actually see them before the high water rages. I'll often mark these structures on a map so I have a better idea where to begin when the water rises. Without having these

structures marked on a map, recalling their location and features is very difficult once they are submerged. The amount of detail you forget is amazing. Slower current breaks during low water become well defined with higher waters. Lower water spots become engulfed with heavy current overnight and push fish into new areas, then those new areas turn red hot overnight.

There is far more to fishing the raging water other than finding good structure. Locating good high water fishing spots also means considering the speed of the water. Several of the bridge pillars look like great hideouts, but in reality there is too little current break during the higher water. The main current during the flood stages is far too fast. These areas are often places that fish don't hang out during higher water. Additionally, venturing into these areas during high water periods can be far too dangerous. On the other hand, eddies that are very slow have a tendency to hold more carp then walleye. These might be fun to catch on a slow day, but I'd rather search for the elusive high water walleye.

The flow of the current plays a large role in river fishing. When the water level rises to the flood stages the strong current will push walleye out of the main channel. This causes walleye to push into areas providing current breaks, often along the shoreline behind newly submerged structure. This structure provides a break from the heavy current in the main channel. As the current flow decreases, walleye return to traditional locations. Tracking locations that are good during different water levels provides a fisherman with fishing options for any river condition.

Spawning walleye have a tremendous urge to move upstream during the spring months, with the rush of the higher water giving the walleye staging at the mouth of the river the opportunity to make this move. When the river rises at a rapid rate the fishing is always slows down. Rising waters scatter walleye into new areas but once the river has crested fish settle back into pockets.

Watching others fish is a great way to learn more about the great sport. When I saw a fisherman using over an ounce of weight on a Carolina rig I initially thought he was crazy. I watched this skillful fisherman as he landed a number of fish, far more than anyone in the vicinity. I asked him several questions about his gear because I was

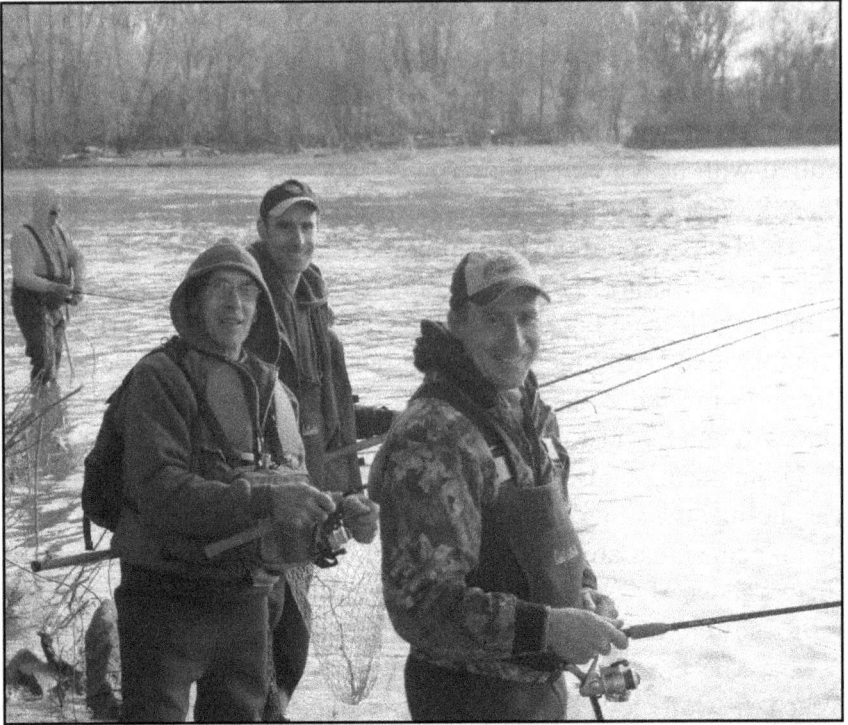

Two generations of the Miller family are working hard during a cold front to land a few walleye. Heavy weight and slower presentation prevailed to complete several limits.

intrigued about his success. He explained the need to slowly ease his jig into a specific hole to entice the fish into biting. I was more concerned with gathering some of his knowledge rather than fishing myself. While standing near him fishing, I stacked several bullet weights together to get an ounce. He was right. This spot required a heavy weight to slow the jig enough to lure the fish into striking. Visibility was reduced to below an inch and slow presentation was needed. Under high water conditions, it is necessary to slow down the presentation since walleye are often not chasing baits.

Water temperature is one of the biggest indicators for spawning walleye; this is a big deal in the spring. A decrease of just a couple degrees can stall any feeding activity. Spring is a time to break free from Mother Nature's frosty grip. The average April temperature is 48°F, but at this time of the year the temperature can vary greatly. Believe it or not, the record high temperature for April was 89°F, set back in 1942, and the record low was a freezing 8°F in 1982. That is a wide variance of temperature. In contrast to this wide range, the target water temperature for spawning is 42-46°F. Cold fronts have dramatic impacts on the water temperature. A drop in temperature of a few degrees will show a noticeably slower walleye bite. Cloudy days, cold nights, and/or cold rain or snow can quickly drop the water temperature. On the contrary, mild evenings combined with sunny days really help bring the temperature back up and spark activity.

Think back a few years ago, I can remember one of the worst cold fronts in the last decade. After hitting an extraordinarily warm late March and early April we got slapped with a hard frost. It not only turned off the bite but also ruined that year's acorn and apple production. For thirteen days straight the temperature was unseasonably cold. When the water temperature dips, the fish remain in the river system but they are inactive. This cold front nearly stopped all walleye feeding activity during those two weeks.

This is all good information, but as a dedicated fisherman I don't hang up the towel during high water or cold weather. This is the time to start fishing in new ways to increase your strikes. Getting into a fish's face will prevail. The longer you can keep a lure in the walleye's strike zone, the better the chance that he will strike the lure. Such conditions always begin by slowing down my retrieval. This can be done by bulking up the weight to slow down your lure, giving it a chance to hang in the strike zone longer. Walleye can be one of the most finicky eaters; cold water that looks like chocolate milk doesn't help matters. A sluggish bite often means nearly hitting a walleye on the nose to get a strike.

Putting together color combinations that are visible in mucky water will help walleye see your lure from a greater distance. Several great color choices are chartreuse, green, orange, pink, and red. These baits can be seen by walleye at greater distances.

High water conditions can be dangerous with the added turbulence. Submerged ditches, unseen brush and trees covered by the dirty water, and large pieces of debris floating downstream are just a few of the hazards. This is a time to be extra careful and strap on

High water often causes fresh walleye to surge into the river. New walleye are more pale (white) and as they reside in the river for a few days they begin to get more color. This will help determine if a new run of walleye has arrived.

a lifejacket. Boating and wading the river can also be difficult during higher water conditions. Given those warnings, there are several islands along the river that offer phenomenal fishing during a transitional water level phase. When the water is slightly too high to access Blue Grass Island, a canoe or kayak has given me access by letting me boat across the channel. I never take to the main current during the flood stage. This is not advisable.

Adding a final touch will help you build a perfect high water strategy: scent! Scent will both help cause more strikes and make fish hang on longer. Holding power allows a fisherman to feel more finicky strikes. I like to use either scent-impregnated lures, spray-on scent, or other salty lures. Lures impregnated with scent trick a walleye to hang on slightly longer, giving fishermen a higher hook set ratio. Inactive fish often suck in the lure and don't run. Therefore many fishermen don't even know there is a walleye holding onto their lure. I use scent any time fishing gets tough because those couple extra seconds are significant. I also use scent when live bait is not allowed on the Maumee River during March or April.

As the water begins to fall, fish that were originally washed into the backwaters start pushing back into traditional walleye structure. This is when life in the river structure begins to return to normal. Working from the shoreline outward helps reveal where the fish are staging. With falling water, these traditional spots mean increasing jig weight to slow the presentation because the current is still very fast. Increasing weights on Carolina rigs upward TO 1-2 ounces may be necessary although extreme. Match the weight to current and only use what is needed. Too heavy a weight causes the lure to slow down too much, and too light a weight means the lure floats above the strike zone. I am consistently amazed that the difference 1/8 oz can have on lure speed, which is fundamental to a successful high water fisherman.

Target the right location with a solid presentation and you are bound to land a stringer of walleye. The longer I walleye fish the more I realize there are always fish biting. Often the bite will slow down, but putting together a high water plan will have you fishing while others are left behind. Rise to the occasion and learn how to catch walleye under adverse conditions.

Chapter 12

Spawn Phases

When breaking the walleye run into periods there are three distinct timeframes: pre-spawn, spawn, and post-spawn. Understanding habits and preferred structure for each of these periods will aid a fisherman in capitalizing on the entire season. Walleye begin to migrate into the Western Basin of Lake Erie during September and October. After the ice breaks up and the water temperature pushes above 30 degrees, fish begin moving into the river.

PRE-SPAWN

During the early pre-spawn periods, walleye slowly begin to stage into the spawning grounds. Many of the local fish are the first to arrive before the main run in March, a secret of the local fishermen. Then as the month of March progresses there will be a substantial amount of walleye migrating up the river system. As the month progresses the spring spawning occurs only when the daylight hours, water temperature, and river flow are right.

Walleye fishing during the run is an exciting time, with so much activity concentrated in one specific location. Each day as the water continues to warm and the water level rises, walleye push into the river and stage near their spawning grounds. During the pre-spawn, the water temperature plays an important role. Cold fronts or cold rain that greatly decrease the water temperature are common, and walleye react strongly to drops in temperature.

When staging during the pre-spawn period, walleye move into deep holes around the spawning grounds. The first walleye to arrive are males. Once they move in, the bite will be very aggressive during warmer weather, while colder weather will turn the bite off. With the weather changing daily, this time can be feast or famine, with walleye feeding patterns responding quickly to the shifting weather.

Following the arrival of the males, a surge of females runs up the river. I have found this short window of opportunity provides the best chance to catch a large female walleye. When they move into the river their eggs are still hard, and they are not ready to spawn. Then, as daylight hours, water temperature, and river flow reach the right level, their eggs soften and they are ready to spawn.

Walleye move more actively during low light conditions, like when the sun is on the horizon and light reflects off the water's surface instead of penetrating it. When the sun is directly overhead, it penetrates deeper into the water with less reflection. Some of the best fishing is available during morning and afternoon hours when the light is significantly reduced. Cloud cover also has a significant effect on light penetration, extending the length of the morning and afternoon bite.

In fishing, I feel there is a learning curve that never really ends. For this reason, I try to surround myself with some of the best fishermen on the Maumee River. While I am confident these men and women can out-fish anyone out there, each one of them is humble about their skill, loves to just fish, and is willing to teach others. I am telling you this because we are always working together to help each other during tough times.

No matter how good you become, there will be tough fishing years. I had one of those years and a good friend pulled me out of my rut. His strategy for catching more pre-spawn walleye is to follow them into the river. Certain sections will be better earlier and later in the pre-spawn period as walleye move into the river. The fish might be biting in those first few days, but you have to find their hiding spots. Once located, they will move. Follow the fish upstream into different areas. Also, remember to slow down the presentation in cold water or early season.

Engbretson Underwater Photography

Walleye surge upstream several times throughout the walleye run. Fishing can drastically improve within hours after fresh schools of walleye enter the river system.

SPAWNING PERIOD

When walleye begin to spawn, they have other things on their minds and are not interested in eating. Luckily for fishermen the spawning period is relatively short. The right temperature for spawning is 40 to 52 degrees, with most Maumee River walleye spawning between 42-46 degrees.

The Maumee River is an ideal spawning ground because of its rocky bottom. The cobblestone rocks scattered across the bottom make some of the best locations to disperse eggs. When the female walleye begin to spawn, they move onto the shallow reefs and riffle to broadcast their eggs. This occurs over a few hours, most often during the evening. Walleye are not interested in eating during the spawning period. Fortunately, not all walleye spawn at the exact same time. Several different groups of new walleye push into the spawning grounds throughout the season. Each of these groups will be in a different period: pre-spawn, spawn, and post-spawn. So this does not mean walleye cannot be caught while a group is spawning;

it simply means targeting those fish in the pre-spawn or post-spawn periods.

The spawn is a unique opportunity to see walleye during daylight in very shallow water. If you catch this right, you can see walleye moving through and rolling in the shallows. I distinctly remember a day I was having a tough time connecting with some walleye. As I moved around, I stopped in a section full of shallow riffles. For half an hour I fished, watching walleye move through the area without touching my jig. This was a great time to actually see walleye rolling in the shallow water while spawning.

The spawning period is tough to fish. Fortunately, several runs of fish move into the river during the spring, so not all are spawning at the same time. Continuing to focus on pre-spawn locations is the best way to approach this challenging phase.

POST-SPAWN

During the heat of the walleye run, many fishermen like me are hitting the shorelines every day. The walleye are stacked in the water and everyone along the river is catching fish. Walleye activity is at its peak and the river is full of fishermen traveling from afar. Then, just as quickly as the walleye filled the rich stretches of the river, they leave and head back to Lake Erie. The intensity falls and the shoreline that was once filled with fishermen is now vacant. The phase of the run changes to the post-spawn and fishing becomes much more difficult.

After going through such an intense peak period it is hard for many to fall into the post-spawn period. Most fishermen put their waders away and wait until next year's walleye run. Those few who are still hungry for walleye action continue to chase the walleye into the later phases.

Many hardcore fishermen know about this period, but no one ever seems to write about it. You hear rumors and stories that many have tried and have had little luck. Understanding the post-spawn period and what happens during this phase will help you become a better fisherman after the crowds have left the banks. Each year is very different, and this period is either amazing or just a blip on the radar. The weather can be the biggest contributing factor to what kind of year it will be.

The Maumee River has the ideal spawning ground because of the cobblestone rocks that scatter along the river floor.

As the season progresses, there are several runs of both male and female walleye that move up stream. Not all walleye spawn at the same time; spawn is a progression throughout the month of April. The final schools of female walleye usually spawn out during late April and head back to the Great Lakes. Female walleye almost immediately return to the Great Lakes after they are spawned out. Once this occurs, the male walleye inhabit the river for up to another month. While some males leave immediately, others stage in the river to recover. This post-spawn period can be boom or bust. The males begin eating again but are targeting smaller baits than during pre-spawn. As the days progress the feeding increases. During this time some of the male walleye begin to migrate back towards the lake. The remaining males seem to go on a feeding frenzy.

After the spawn, walleye move off the spawning grounds and begin to recuperate from the tough spawning period. They move into nearby areas where they can feed in the calmer waters, with deep holes and current breaks as their ideal locations. The male walleye will often stay in the river for weeks before retreating back to Lake Erie, but can be difficult to fish as they disperse throughout the river system.

I will never forget the lesson I learned in early May during a low water year. I found a very small hole that was stacked with walleye, but navigating into position was tortuous. This part of the river has many shelves that can easily drop-off several feet. With water creeping dangerously close to the top of my waders, I spent over 30 minutes taking baby steps across the river to get into position. But once there, the action lit up like fireworks on the Fourth of July. Just about every other cast found me landing another walleye. One after another perfect frying sized walleye fell into my hands. I reached my limit in short order, then spent the next hours in bliss, catching and releasing another two dozen.

All walleye do not spawn at the same time therefore pre-spawn walleye can be targeted for a significant portion of the season. Brian Miller, Connie Ledwidge, and Tim Smojver enjoy a successful afternoon.

I proceeded to return to the scene of the crime for more action over the next five days. On the fifth day I convinced my father to join me. He is not much for wading carelessly across the river, but after strapping on our life jackets we headed to the honey hole. I'm glad we had the opportunity, because it was memorable to see my father take his first limit of walleye ever. In the short time that we fished he also landed his largest walleye ever, but unfortunately my hand full of thumbs lost it at the net. I've lost many of my own walleye and never worried too much about it. But losing another person's fish always bothers me.

This post-spawn phase of the run was simply amazing. These fish were so aggressive that in the frenzy of activity we saw other walleye following our lures up to us several times. In this five day

period there were several occasions when I'd landed doubles on my combo rig. I don't know about you, but prior to this day the only time I've landed two or more fish is when I'm pan fishing. If this ever happens, relish the moment. It doesn't happen often. Walleye run in schools so it's possible to land two walleye when running two lures, but it is still uncommon. From that year going forward, I have targeted walleye during the post-spawn phases.

Until May, the Ohio Department of Natural Resources (ODNR) has regulations on hook size, single hooks, and fishing times. According to the ODNR, the following regulations are in effect from March 1 to May 1:

- Fishing is allowed from sunrise to sunset only in the Maumee River from the Ohio Turnpike bridge to the Old Waterville interurban bridge at the end of Forst Road in Wood County and from the St. Rt. 578 bridge to the Grand Rapids Providence dam.
- No fishing with a line with more than a single hook. The line may not have a hook larger than one-half inch from shank to point, or lure having more than a single hook larger than one-half inch from shank to point
- Treble hooks are prohibited.

Please see the www.ohiodnr.com for a full set of regulations. The regulations noted above are effective as of 2012 and are subject to change.

Starting in May all the prior regulations are lifted, making it possible to use multiple hooks and to fish in the evening. These seem like simple changes, but with lifted regulations the fishing lures and techniques blow wide open. Many fishermen begin using multiple jigs, suspending minnows, inline spinners, and even live minnows. Once the single hook regulation is no longer in effect, some of the local favorites are smaller crankbaits. Anything that looks like a small shiner is effective. If you are confident with the fishing technique, then use it. With the regulations opening up, I've often found this part of the year to be very enjoyable.

After the main period of the run many fishermen disband. With more room between fishermen, using different techniques becomes much easier. At this time of the year I tend to fish like I'm targeting smallmouth, drastically downsizing both my equipment

During the post-season walleye disperse and begin to recover. This is a great time to use canoes to reach secluded holes that have not received much fishing pressure. Once walleye are located, action can quickly pick up.

and my lures. There is also more time spent running and gunning along the river. At this time I am searching for schools of walleye before they leave the river. One of my biggest secrets during May is using small panfish size lures down to 1/16 oz jig. I have even been known to use small crappie fuzzy grubs or one inch grub tails. Downsizing to this degree has given me great successes during this time of the year. A smaller bait presentation is necessary to capitalize on the remaining male walleye. Some fishermen in the Maumee employ these sizes throughout the year with great success. For some reason, these tiny baits work wonders for the walleye during the

After the intense peak it is hard for many to fish the post-spawn period therefore it is often overlooked.

late portions of the season. Most often I'll stack up to three small jigs, tripling my chances for success. I've even run a lead jig with a floating jig trailing behind. This allows you to fish two slightly different columns of water with two different presentations.

Once the walleye have completed spawning, the water temperature continues to rise. The warmer temperature brings on the spawning of white bass. These bass quickly fill up the river in swarms, but among the white bass there are still many walleye to be caught. However, many fishermen think the arrival of the white bass signifies the end of the walleye run. Overnight, the fishing pressure drops dramatically; it doesn't make sense because the river is still full of walleye. The male walleye stay in the river after spawning is complete and start gobbling up food, and because the Maumee River is a tributary to Lake Erie there are many walleye resident in the river year round. It's not the millions that travel up during the spawn, but it's enough to keep me coming back.

The largest change during the post-spawn period is that the walleye begin to transition. I have focused most of my attention on current breaks. Often focusing on one spot will not produce as much as moving into different areas searching for those active walleye. This means moving along the river and fishing lots of different current breaks. Many spots can be hit or miss, so once a high concentration of walleye is located, continue working that area.

The end of the season after the females have left brings on a transitional period, and each day the bite increases. After a long breeding season the male walleye are worn down and need to recuperate. Smaller male walleye tend to recuperate more quickly, which means they will begin biting first. Their appetite continues to increase until they eventually begin eating anything that moves. They get very aggressive, and the bite is on.

Recently, creel limits have increased starting in May. It is a welcome surprise to have perfect eating size walleye hitting hard on anything you toss in front of them. Once I locate a concentration of fish, it's time to continue visiting as many consecutive days as possible. It won't be long before those fish will retreat back towards Lake Erie, so you need to take advantage of the opportunity while it lasts. Experience has taught me to work areas of the river that have not been overfished in the past month. Smaller secluded holes all the way up past Waterville are great when the water is low enough to permit fishing. When higher water prevails, the season often comes to an abrupt halt, with the higher water washing many of the males back into Lake Erie.

For most of the season a medium action rod is appropriate, but during low water conditions a medium-light action can be better. Downgrading equipment size has helped me capitalize on all the finesse techniques described above.

The late season comes with lighter crowds and more ability to move from location to location. One of my favorite pastimes is taking to the water in a canoe or kayak to tackle some of those undisturbed holes. Parts of the river are difficult to access because of private land. Maneuvering into these locations with a canoe makes it easy to jump from location to location. There have been many times I used the canoe to gain access, then anchored the boat and wader fished. This gives me both the access to the area and the flexibility to move into different locations without managing the canoe.

I have enjoyed good luck luring smaller male walleye, the type that makes a wonderful shoreline dinner, during lower water conditions. The many holes along the river offer the opportunity to move from location to location until you find what you're looking for. This time of the year it's important to follow the fish as they retreat back toward the lake. The post-spawn can be boom or bust. A late rain and high waters will quickly ruin the hot action by pushing the walleye back into Lake Erie just as quickly as they entered. Alternately, steady water levels will keep those male feeding on minnows to recoup. I have had many May successes, making this phase high on my hit list. When it all comes together, those hours spent on the river will not soon be forgotten.

Chapter 13

Trophy Walleye

The Maumee River provides some of the greatest opportunities to catch a trophy walleye. The pre-spawn period is the best time to target walleye over 28 inches long. Each year I see a few walleye stretching beyond 30 inches. We have rich waters that produce healthy walleye throughout the Great Lakes. Walleye in the northern regions of the United States grow much larger than those in southern regions. Walleye in the northern regions grow at a slower rate and have a longer lifespan. Some of the Northern region states include Ohio, Michigan, and Minnesota.

Before understanding how to target trophy walleye we are going to review the Lake Erie Walleye Growth Charts. These studies review conducted by the ODNR Fisheries Biologist include walleye from 2004-2009 seasons. The sample size was over 6,000 walleye. During the study, the fish were grouped into male and female groups. Also there are a number of fish which the gender was not determined therefore they were categorized in the "All Fish" sample. This makes the all fish sample a larger sampling.

Some very interesting facts transpired when taking a deeper look at the walleye growth rates. In the sample there was one female walleye with the lifespan of 26 years. This is a rare opportunity, the oldest walleye sampled from any ODNR Fisheries Biologist. On the oldest end of the sample spectrum were nine walleye at 22 years old, one at 24 years old, and one at 26 years old. Female walleye grow faster and longer than male walleye. At 10 years, female walleye averaged 27.3 inches; male walleye average 22.7 inches. Where this helps me the greatest is to understand the range of walleye by age. Following are two graphs that cover these details; mean age by inch group and mean length at age. Both are provided by the Travis Hartman ODNR Fisheries Biologist.

Jeff Miller holds up a respectable 27 inch walleye caught in the early spring.

Brian Miller caught a big 28 inch walleye during mid-April.

After reviewing the ODNR Fisheries Biologist research provided, it is obvious that female walleye grow faster and longer. From their sample the longest male walleye was 28 inches; the longest female walleye was a whopping 31 inches long.

The Maumee River is the largest tributary to Lake Erie with masses of walleye rushing upstream during the spring run. In Lake Erie many of the larger walleye move back to the Western Basin during the fall to stage for the spring spawning season. Through nighttime studies, the Fisheries Biologist has reported many trophy size walleye in the Maumee River during the spring. This is the perfect opportunity for fisherman to catch a trophy.

The most important factor for any trophy hunter is to fish where trophy fish are present. You cannot catch a fish that does not live in the water you are fishing, from the ODNR studies we know trophy walleye exist in Lake Erie. Many of those big fish enter the tributaries to spawn providing an even better opportunity for river fishermen. Now that we know big fish exist in the river it time to focus on big fish locations within the river to capitalize. There are different techniques to catching quality over quantity.

To target larger walleye, it makes sense to focus on female walleye. Females are less prevalent and prefer different types of structure and current. More than ever big walleye are nocturnal. They tend to hold in slack water and deep holes, Often there is a strong current area through the rapids then deeper slow water. The slow water areas near structure are big fish locations.

The presentation has to slow and takes more time. It is about working quality water for bigger fish therefore taking far fewer bites. During higher water trophies are pushed closer to the riprap, in slow churning eddies, and in the rocks. Often they hold back farther in the deep pools of water.

Females arrive in the river and begin to ripen. This period is short lived. Once a female is spawned out she retreats back into Lake Erie almost immediately. There is a short period that trophy

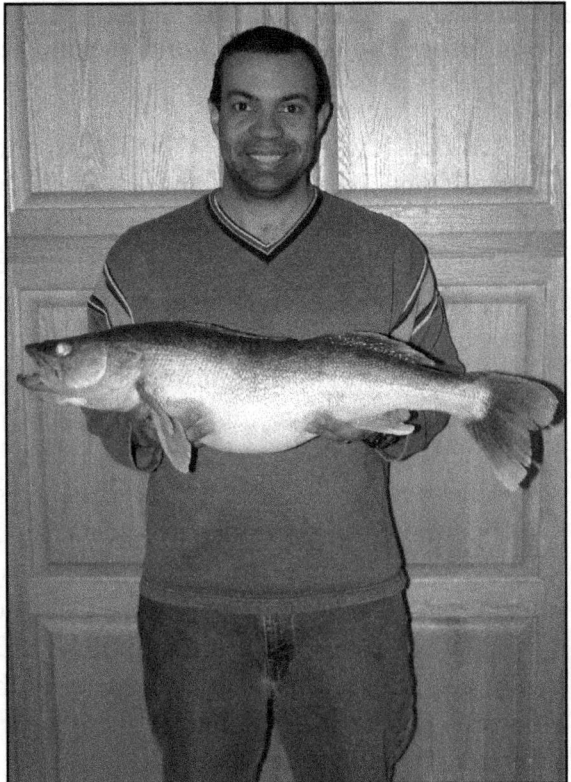

Rich Nicholas proudly shows his 30 inch, 10 lb trophy walleye. He is a dedicated walleye fisherman that chases them year-round.

fishing for walleye is at its best. Once a female is spawning she wants nothing to do with eating. Then during the post-spawn she is recuperating and does not eat like during the pre-spawn. Often by the time she really begins eating again she is already in Lake Erie.

My disclaimer is that any location can produce a large walleye. To focus on the majority of the big fish is to fish from the tip of Blue Grass Island and downstream. The majority of females are in those areas. The farther downstream through Orleans Park are ideal locations. Look over the river for the deepest holes and slower water adjacent to current. That makes a winning location.

Trophy fishing is exciting. I love seeing the pole bend over and pull back to feel a lug on the other end. There is nothing like catching a few big walleyes each year. Trophy fishing is just that, searching out the biggest walleyes in the river. It is exhilarating to land a walleye over 28 inches. In the end most of the trophy walleye I catch get released back for another day. A quick picture and memory will last a lifetime. A measurement and picture is enough for any taxidermist to produce a replica for the den. Those 18 to 24 inch male walleye are the perfect size for eating. Anything bigger and the meat does not taste like the high-quality filets I typically get.

Lake Erie Walleye: Mean Age by Inch Group

All Fish

	Inch Group																
	15	16	17	18	19	20	21	22	23	24	25	26	27	28	29	30	31
Min. Age	2	2	2	2	3	3	3	4	4	5	5	6	7	8	8	10	12
Avg. Age	2.5	3	3.6	4	4.7	5.3	6	6.8	7.6	8.1	8.7	9.9	11	13	13	14	15
Max. Age	4	6	6	8	9	16	24	21	22	26	22	20	22	22	22	21	19
Sample Size	309	402	579	595	621	757	607	507	410	287	233	174	211	167	85	49	10

Males

	Inch Group																
	15	16	17	18	19	20	21	22	23	24	25	26	27	28	29	30	31
Min. Age	2	2	2	3	3	4	3	4	6	6	10	11					
Avg. Age	2.7	3.1	3.8	4.3	5.3	6.2	7.5	9.8	12	12	13	15					
Max. Age	4	6	6	8	9	16	15	21	22	21	20	20	22	17			
Sample Size	192	248	334	331	297	327	198	149	97	55	20	3		1			

Females

	Inch Group																
	15	16	17	18	19	20	21	22	23	24	25	26	27	28	29	30	31
Min. Age	2	2	2	2	3	3	3	4	4	5	5	6	7	8	8	10	13
Avg. Age	2.3	2.7	3	3.3	4	4.4	4.9	5.4	6	7.1	8.3	9.9	12	13	14	14	16
Max. Age	3	6	6	5	6	7	9	10	13	26	22	22	22	22	22	21	19
Sample Size	46	72	140	157	214	272	295	289	253	185	168	144	185	153	74	41	7

Travis Hartman ODNR Fisheries Biologist

Lake Erie Walleye: Mean Length at Age

All Fish

	2	3	4	5	6	7	8	9	10	11	12	13	14	15	16	17	18	19	20	21	22	23	24	25	26
Min. Length	15	15	15.2	16.2	16	19	19	20	20	20	20	20	21	21	20	23	22	23	23	27	27				25
Avg. Length	16	18	19.2	21	22	23	24	25	26	25	27	26	27	28	27	28	28	27	27	27	27				25
Max. Length	19	22	23.2	25.5	27	28	29	30	31	31	31	32	31	32	31	31	31	31	30	31	31				25
Sample Size	337	837	1,258	1,055	772	310	351	207	216	148	124	127	86	50	31	18	23	17	15	10	9				1

Age

Males

	2	3	4	5	6	7	8	9	10	11	12	13	14	15	16	17	18	19	20	21	22	23	24	25	26
Min. Length	15	15	15.2	16.2	16	19	19	20	20	20	20	20	21	20	21	23	22	24	23	24	24				
Avg. Length	16	17	18	19.4	20	21	22	22	23	23	23	23	23	24	23	24	22	24	25	24	25				
Max. Length	18	22	22.3	23	25	23	25	25	25	26	26	26	27	26	26	28	24	25	27	24	28				
Sample Size	135	421	439	398	304	112	133	50	59	56	31	44	25	12	11	6	1	5	5	4	2				

Age

Females

	2	3	4	5	6	7	8	9	10	11	12	13	14	15	16	17	18	19	20	21	22	23	24	25	26
Min. Length	15	15	16.2	17.9	17	20	21	22	22	24	24	26	26	28	28	26	29	30	31	30	31				25
Avg. Length	17	18	20.2	22.1	23	25	26	27	27	27	28	28	29	29	28	30	29	29	29	28	28				25
Max. Length	19	21	23.2	25.5	27	28	29	30	31	31	30	32	31	32	31	31	31	31	30	31	31				25
Sample Size	91	327	462	537	340	159	140	121	134	75	75	66	51	35	16	11	22	11	9	5	7				1

Age

Travis Hartman ODNR Fisheries Biologist

Chapter 14

Fishing Locations

One of the biggest questions I get asked from anglers is where should I fish today. I am guilty of asking the same question myself. Understanding where to fish on any given day has a lot to do with daily weather conditions, river height, and run timing. This book has been designed to help answer those questions and place you in the right location each time you take to the water. After understanding how walleye relate to structure during different periods of the season and walleye patterns will begin to evolve. These patterns help you understand where to fish on any given day of the season.

We are blessed to have fishing accessible throughout the entire tributary. During the spring run, walleye can swim upstream until they reach Providence Dam. Throughout this stretch of river there are many access points providing excellent fishing opportunities. Once you have become versed in the most popular locations then explore a few of those less popular locations. These will be less crowded yet offer some excellent fishing experiences. I will discuss a few of the most popular access points and boat launches. There are more access locations along the river, only those most visited are

Some of the best locations are off the normal path. Use your wall-eye knowledge to discover new killer locations.

listed. Each has some unique structure but once the river increases above the normal level, many of these access points are unfishable because of unsafe conditions.

The Ohio Department of Natural Resources (ODNR) indicates, caution is strongly recommended in rivers as they are often high in the early spring and quite treacherous. Please use caution and follow the ODNR's safety advice whenever accessing the river. If you do not feel safe then do not access the river regardless.

Following are a couple notes about the details provided below. Many refer to the river as the Maumee, Ohio or Perrysburg, Ohio side of the river. I will provide an address or riverside along with Global Positioning Satellite (GPS) coordinates. Additionally there will be notes to public and private access points along the river. Private land can still be fished if it is accessed by the waterway.

Orleans Park

ACCESS: Public Access with Boat Launch
LOCATION: 655 Maumee Western Reserve Perrysburg, Ohio 43551
COUNTY: Wood County
LATITUDE: 41.5569961
LONGITUDE: -83.6449353

WATER LEVEL WARNING: Orleans Park can be fished during various water levels. This includes times when other locations are closed due to higher water levels.

FISHING EXPERIENCE: Access to Orleans Park is off Front Street within Perrysburg, Ohio. There is a mixture of rock piles, large rocks mixed with a rocky bottom, and some deep pools. Many fishermen target the section downstream from the boat launch. There is an impressive view of Audubon Islands Nature Preserve, some fisherman use small boats to access the fishing on and around those islands. This section of the river widens therefore the current slows down even during high water periods.

On the downstream side of the Conant Street Bridge is another excellent location with a good mixture of rocks and rip-rap. This location is heavily fished during high water when water height reaches over 583 feet. Additionally, there is a boat launch located at the park for small boats.

Towpath Park

ACCESS: Public Access
LOCATION: Located at the end of E. Harrison Street and White Street, Maumee Ohio
COUNTY: Lucas County
LATITUDE: 41.5592184
LONGITUDE: -83.6507687

WATER LEVEL WARNING: Towpath Park can be fished during various water levels. This includes times when other locations are closed due to higher water levels.

FISHING EXPERIENCE: The section runs from White Street Access to Conant Street. It is considered the Towpath Park although many local fishing reports specify this access as "White Street Access" and "The Towpath." When the water is high, it pushes walleye against the riprap along the shoreline. Below the Conant Street Bridge is a wider section that slows down during higher water. There are several excellent deep pools, creak inlets, eddies, pilings, and plenty of rocky structure. Along the bottom are big rocks and riprap that provide some outstanding walleye structure.

This area can safely be fished from the shoreline. Use caution when wading, some of the riprap continues to drop off into deep holes. Other portions along this access point level off at the bottom of the riprap with a flat river floor consisting of small pebbles and sand. Along the entire stretch near the towpath be prepared to combat with overgrown brush and low overhanging trees.

The trail runs along the Maumee River from Towpath Park through Side Cut Metropark. The path can be accessed from White Street and Elizabeth Street. There is limited parking at the end of Harrison Street and more parking available along the public streets.

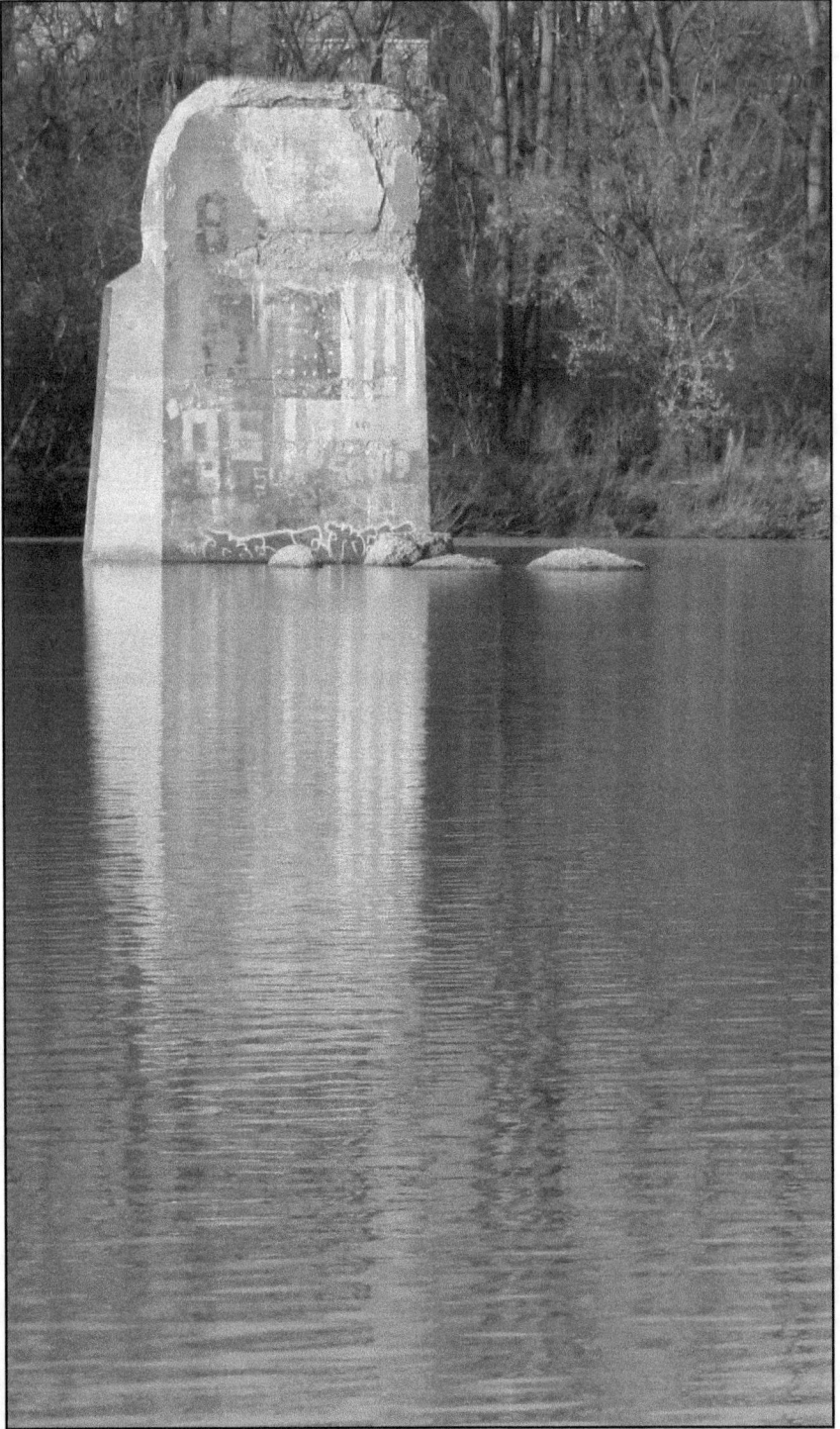

Fort Meigs

ACCESS: Public Access
LOCATION: Located at the end of Rapids Road off Maumee Western Reserve in Perrysburg, Ohio
COUNTY: Wood County
LATITUDE: 41.555092
LONGITUDE: -83.650487

WATER LEVEL WARNING: Fort Meigs can be fished during various water levels. This includes times when other locations are closed due to higher water levels.

FISHING EXPERIENCE: Fort Meigs stands tall bestowing a historic backdrop to the worthy fishing that lies below. The area is rated as a top large walleye location primarily because of the deep holes and slower water. At times this area can generate slower action but that is the trade off for trophy fish. Fishermen can access the entire Perrysburg Ohio side that extends upstream from this access point.

Many target directly in front of the parking lot during higher water periods. When the peninsula is accessible many fishermen access this area to reach the main current. Beyond Fort Meigs the majority of the property is private land but provides excellent rocky bottom structure. The farther you venture upstream, the lighter the fishing pressure.

Ford Street

ACCESS: Public Access
LOCATION: Southern end of Ford Street in Maumee, Ohio
COUNTY: Lucas County
LATITUDE: 41.556276
LONGITUDE: -83.662423

WATER LEVEL WARNING: Ford Street access can be fished during various water levels. As the water levels increase to flood stages this access become unfishable.

FISHING EXPERIENCE: Ford Street access is located downstream from Blue Grass Island. The water sweeps back behind the island across many different shallow riffles. This area has a mixture of rocky bottoms, deep pools, and shallow riffles. There are large subtle eddies that allow walleye to hide from the current. The muddy shoreline drops off quickly so be careful during higher water periods, during lower water this is not a concern.

The channel from Blue Grass Island and the mainstream meet and the river is very wide. When lower water occurs, fishermen will wade throughout this section of the river. During higher water boats scatter below the island along several shallow reefs. The area located along the Metropark trails offers a wonderful view of wildlife and scenery. Parking is only available along the public streets.

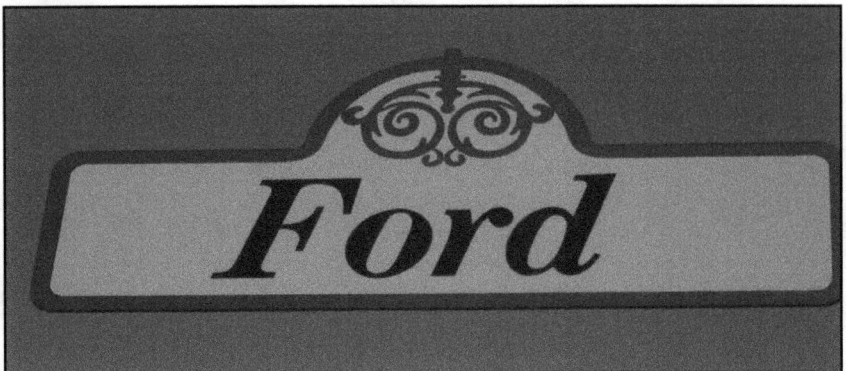

Schroeder Farm Campground

ACCESS: Private Access and Private Boat Launch
LOCATION: 27149-27841 W River Rd, Perrysburg, Ohio 43551
COUNTY: Wood County
LATITUDE: 41.544023
LONGITUDE: -83.669933

WATER LEVEL WARNING: Schroeder Farm Campground access can be fished during various water levels. As the water levels increase to flood stages this access become unfishable.

FISHING EXPERIENCE: This stretch is located on the Perrysburg side across from the East end of Blue Grass Island. There are many deep holes, current breaks and rocky bottom with larger rocks protruding from the river floor. This is across from the mid-section of Blue Grass Island providing a different perspective.

The variety of structure provides a mix of male and female walleye. The fishing pressure is lighter along this stretch during much of the year. There are some deeper sections with ripples both upstream and downstream from the campground. This is an excellent area to catch a mix of large and smaller walleye. Schroeders Farm Campground is privately owned, camping and launching boats require a fee but the waterway is free to access.

SCHROEDER FARM
PARKING ~ CAMPING ~ BOAT LAUNCH
WALLEYE FISHING
PARKING: $5.00
BOAT LAUNCH: $8.00
CAMPING: $15.00
ASK ABOUT WEEKLY
AND MONTHLY PASSES!

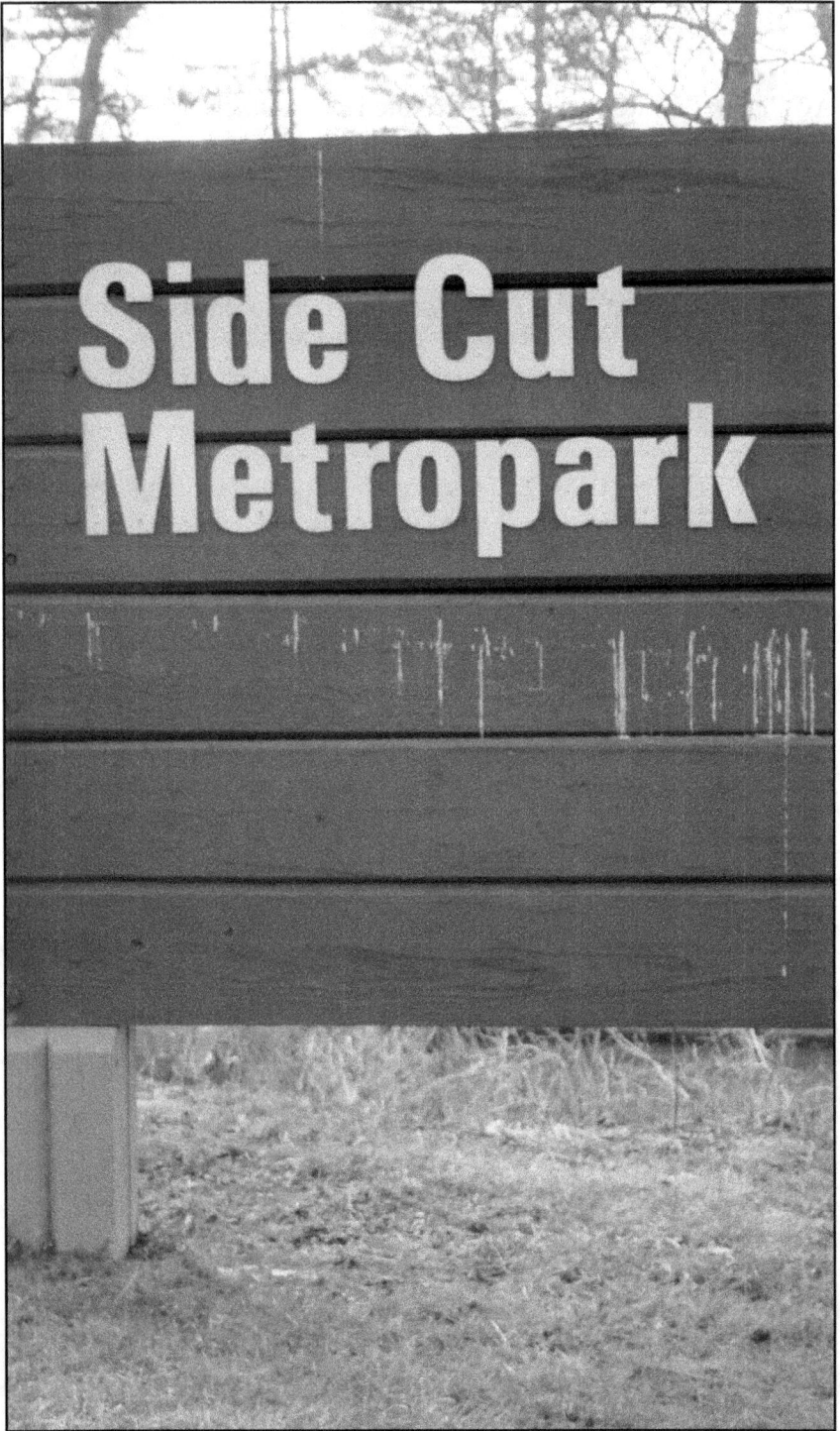

Blue Grass Island

ACCESS: Public Access
LOCATION:1025 River Road, Maumee, Ohio
COUNTY: Lucas County
LATITUDE: 41.5506075
LONGITUDE: -83.671047

WATER LEVEL WARNING: When water levels increase to 582 ft. or above Side Cut Metropark prohibits fishermen from accessing Blue Grass Island by wading.

FISHING EXPERIENCE: Fishing pressure on Blue Grass Island is often heavy during the peak season. This is a very large island and offers a variety of structure. I will divide the island into four large units; upper, mid, lower, and the channel.

The upper section which is farthest upstream has some excellent ripples and rocky structure. Many fishermen extend beyond the front of the island and reach out into the deeper main channel. The mid-section is straight and long with a big area of shallow ripples followed by some deep channels. Towards the tail of the mid-section there is a great turn that provides some good current and deep holes. The turn in the island speeds up the flow of the water. The lower section provides several deep channels, ripples, large rocks, and several calm eddies.

To reach Blue Grass Island you must cross the channel. This area is an under fished section of the river. During transitional water periods walleye are pushed out of the main current and into the channel. Do not overlook this section of protected water. The entire island has some excellent rocky structure. There are some amazing current breaks scattered throughout the island. There are so many good locations scattered throughout each section of the island.

When water levels drop below 580 ft. fishermen from opposing sides of the river wade dangerously close together. To avoid conflict, each side of the river needs to respect those across the river by fishing only their side. During higher water periods fishing alongside of the island with a boat can be great.

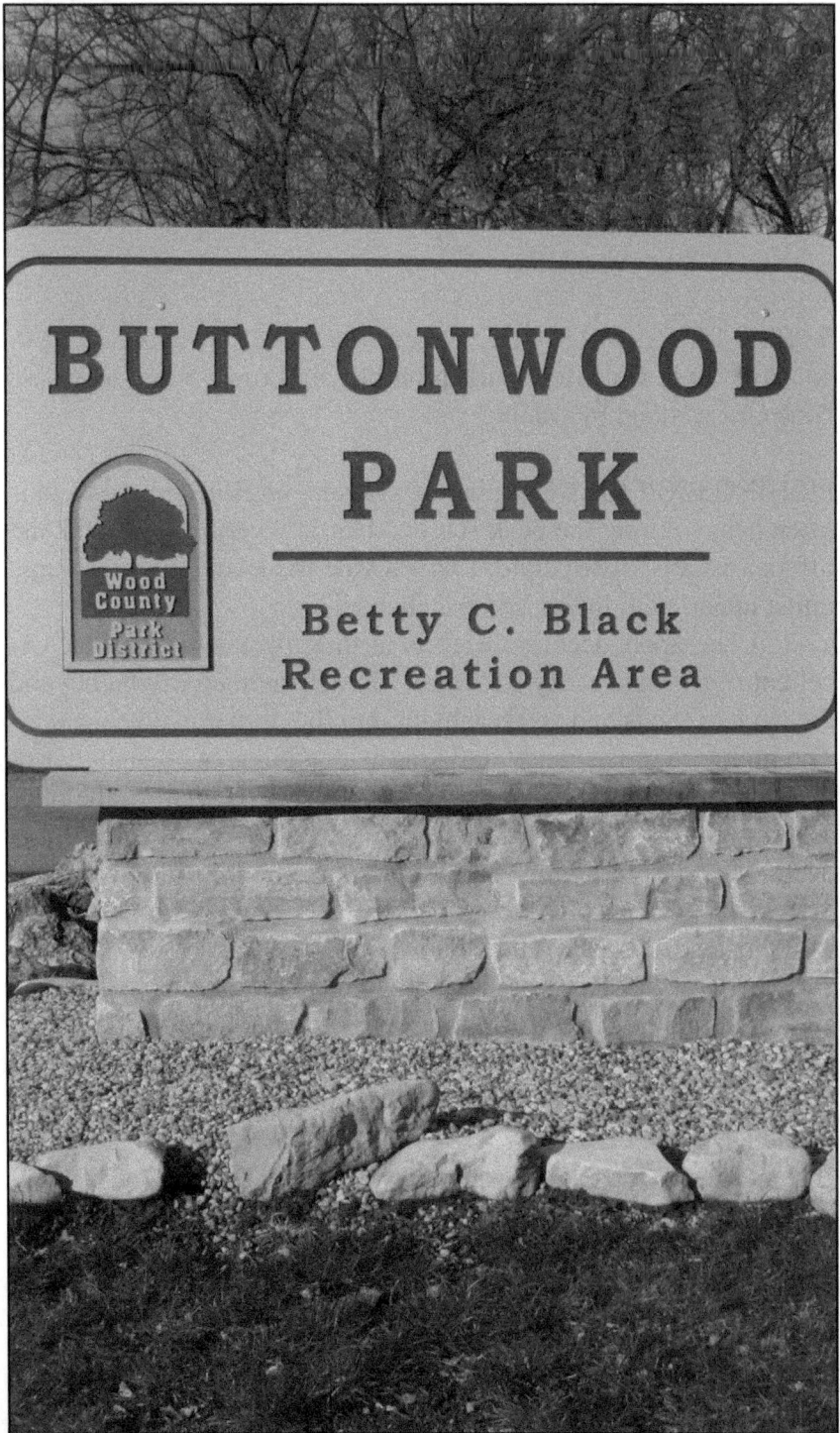

Buttonwood-Betty C Black Recreation Area

ACCESS: Public Access
LOCATION: 27174 Hull Prairie Road Perrysburg, Ohio 43551
COUNTY: Wood County
LATITUDE: 41.5467186
LONGITUDE: -83.6724359

WATER LEVEL WARNING: Buttonwood access can be fished during various water levels. As the water levels increase to flood stages this access become unfishable.

FISHING EXPERIENCE: Fishing pressure is heavy at Buttonwood throughout the year. Directly in front of Hull Prairie Road is a very deep rocky pool of water. Just downstream are two large reefs. During mid-height water (slightly above 582 ft.) fishermen cannot wade to the second reef. Fishing along the shore works well during this stage. Once the water levels decline to normal levels the second reef can be reached with waders.

This section provides an excellent long deep channel and rocky structure. There is a mix of male and female walleye caught along this is area. Some trophy walleye can be caught in this stretch of the river. Finding a place to stand between the chaos can be a challenge, this is a busy section of the river. Good fishing is available during all periods of the walleye run.

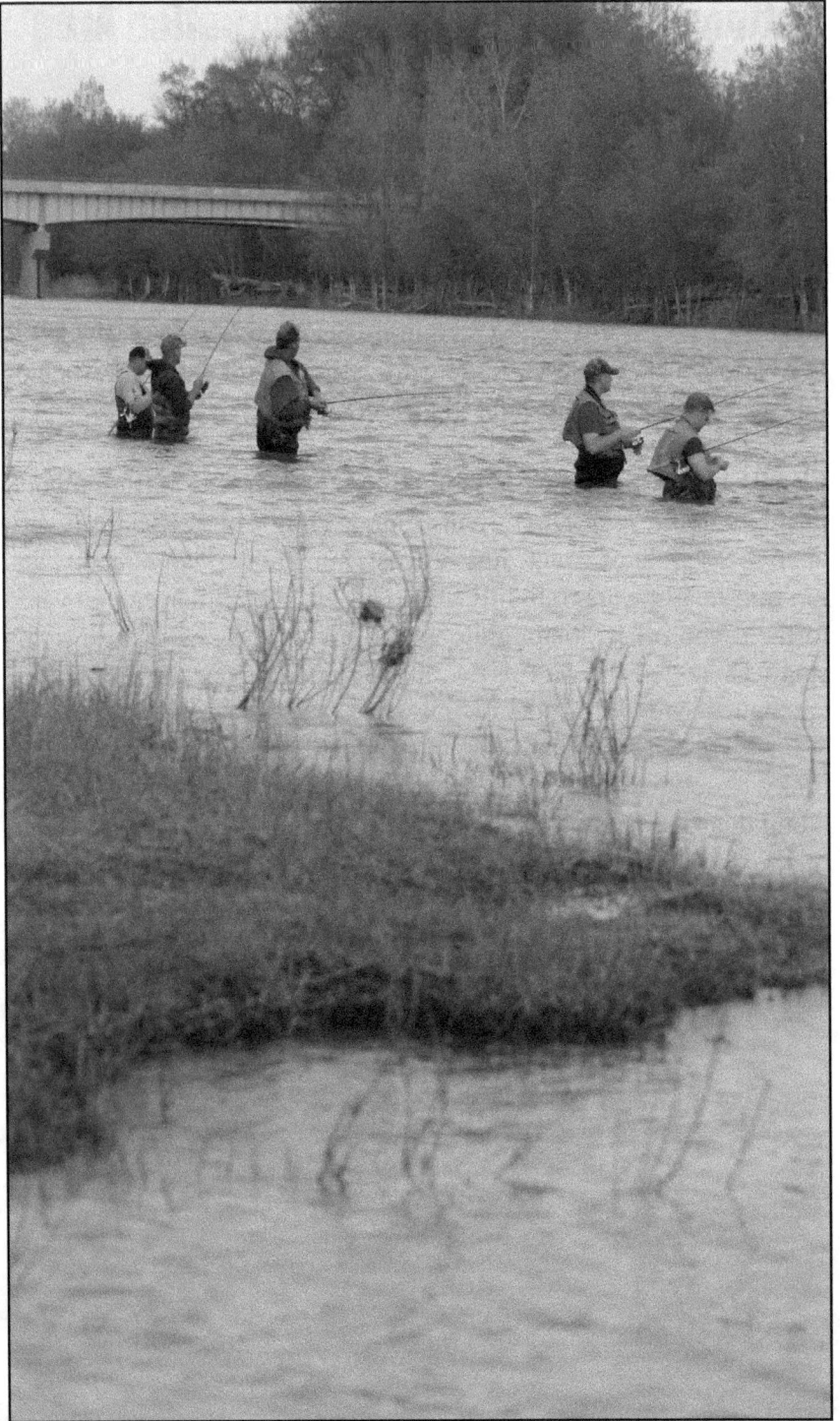

Jerome Road

ACCESS: Public Access
LOCATION: On North River Road between Jerome Road and 475
Bridge in Maumee Ohio
COUNTY: Lucas County
LATITUDE: 41.539952
LONGITUDE: -83.694298

WATER LEVEL WARNING: This entire section above and below the rapids become dangerous when the river rises above normal levels.

FISHING EXPERIENCE: Jerome Road is very easy to access therefore the fishing pressure is quite intense. The best fishing occurs during normal and low water periods. Once the water increases above 582 ft. then caution is needed but fishing can take place as the water increases towards 583 ft. There are several deep holes and main channels towards the center of the river. Below the Fallen Timber Rapids are several holes scattered about. There are so many excellent locations along Jerome Road as many walleye stage throughout the whole section. When the water is higher the current is very fast and a heavier lure weight is needed to slow down the presentation.

This is primarily accessed from Side Cut Metropark because the Perrysburg side is primarily private. However, both sides of the river offer excellent fishing. The Perrysburg Ohio side has some large rocks and deep holes relatively close to shore. The walk is an exceptionally long walk to access those locations unless a canoe is used to cross the river.

Upstream from the rapids, the river floor changes drastically. Shale rock prevails; this causes many sharp drop-offs that create small shelves to hold walleye. Additionally scattered around are deep holes, which are hard to locate by sight. Good knowledge of the river is a must to tackle upstream of the rapids. With less fishing pressure it is ideal for kayaks, canoes or small john boats during low water periods.

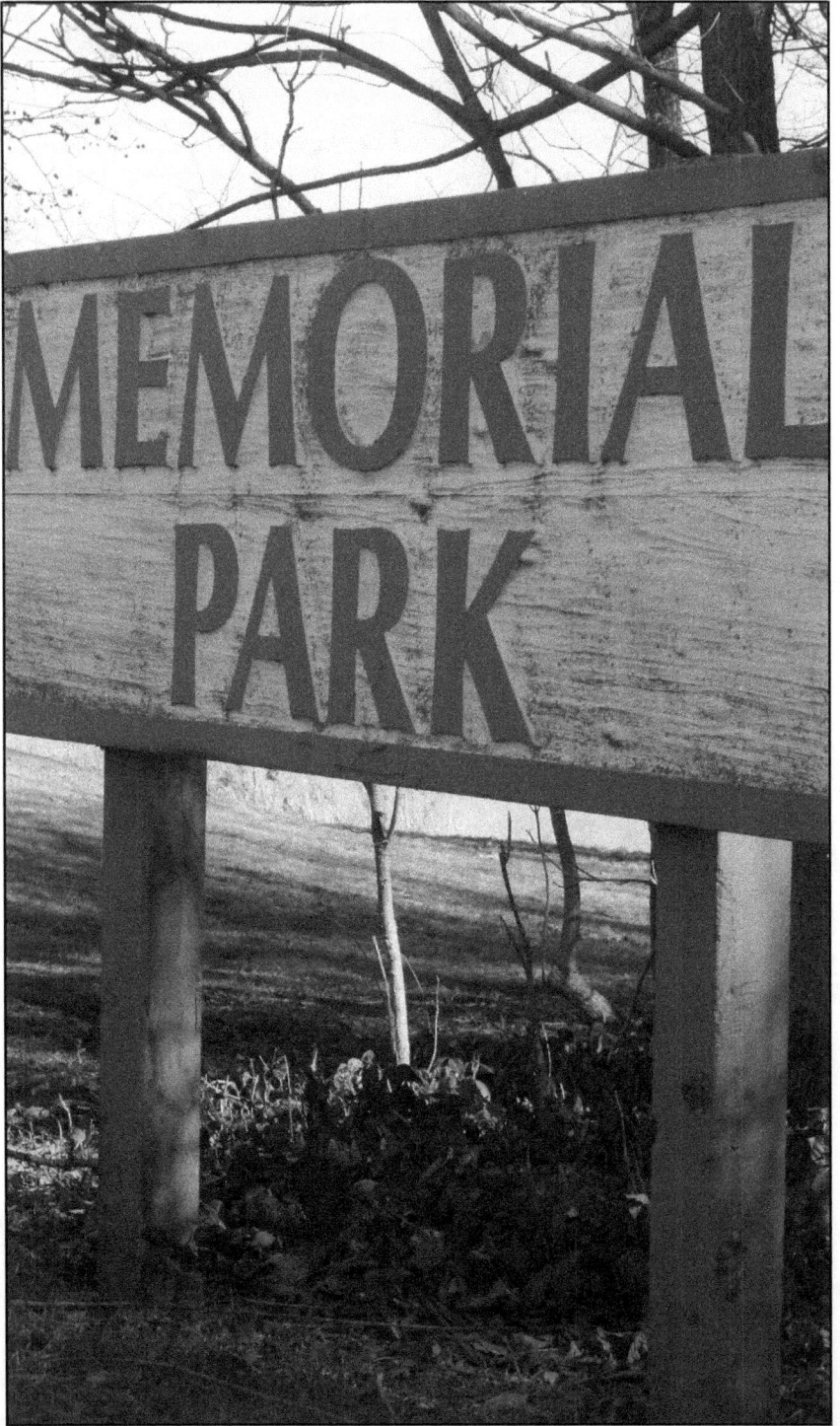

Memorial Park

ACCESS: Public Access
LOCATION: At the end of Water Street just south of the Waterville
Bridge
COUNTY: Lucas County
LATITUDE: 41.499506
LONGITUDE: -83.715734

WATER LEVEL WARNING: This section of the river is best fished
during lower water periods. Any rise above normal water levels
makes this stretch inaccessible and can become dangerous.

FISHING EXPERIENCE: The area I will discuss is the stretch upstream from Jerome Road all the way through Waterville Ohio. The
most popular area in this section of river is the Memorial Park access point. Fishermen scatter throughout this area with the majority
fishing near the rapids at the Waterville Bridge. Many fisherman
cross to the island and fish deeper holes towards the main channel.
Primary structure consists of shale rock with a mix of gravel and
chunk rock. Use caution, there are many quick drop-offs that can be
dangerous to someone unfamiliar with the area.

Many experienced fisherman run and gun this section downstream of the Waterville Bridge to locate hungry male walleyes.
There is a public access at Memorial Park in downtown Waterville
and a small roadside parking lot across the Waterville Bridge for access on the Wood County side of the river. Fishing pressure is much
lighter in this area. This far upstream typically means male walleye
will be your target, not as many females move into this area. Fishing
can be fast and furious. The lighter crowds allow for a more enjoyable experience.

Farnsworth Metropark

ACCESS: Public Access and Boat Launch
LOCATION: 8505 S. River Road (US 24), Waterville, Ohio
COUNTY: Lucas County
LATITUDE: 41.4858859
LONGITUDE: -83.739104

WATER LEVEL WARNING: Wader fishing should only be done during low water periods or boat accessible in the deeper sections.

FISHING EXPERIENCE: As you leave the city of Waterville Ohio, traveling southwest along River Road are expanses of shallower water, excellent for wading. This section is best fished during shallow water periods. The river bottom is shale and chunk rock with many small shelves.

Further upstream near the Farnsworth Boat Launch is a large section of deep water and islands. Some fisherman enjoy launching boats and trolling the deeper pockets for spring walleye. The park overlooks three islands; Missionary, Butler and Indian. Fishing is decent throughout this stretch of deep water but primarily holds male walleye. Fishing pressure is low during all periods of the walleye run.

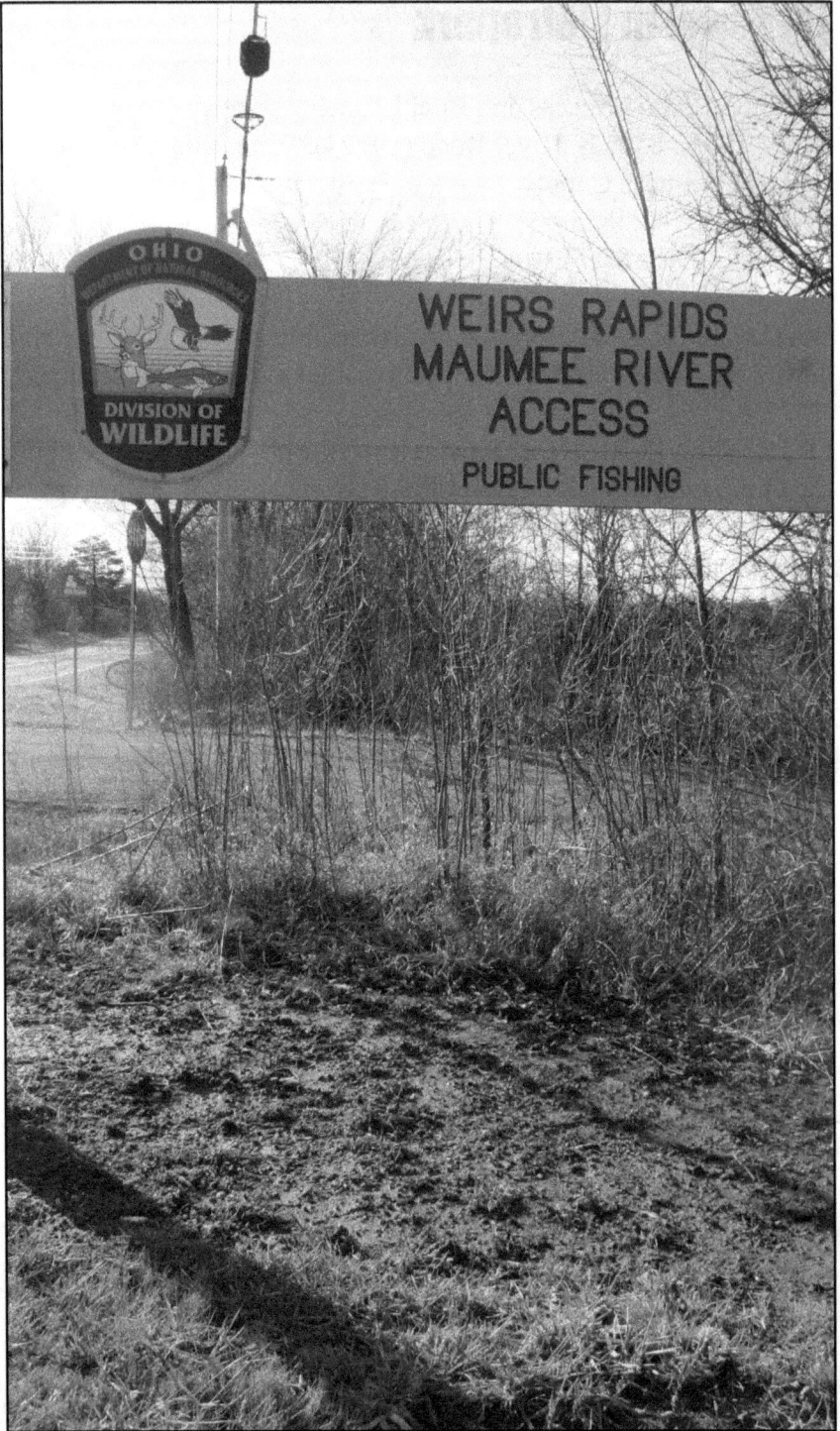

Weirs Rapids

ACCESS: Public Access
LOCATION: Cross the Waterville Bridge (Route 64) towards Wood County. Drive southwest down Route 65 and turn right turn on Range Line Road. There is parking at the end of Range Line Road.
COUNTY: Wood County
LATITUDE: 41.461306
LONGITUDE: -83.766965

WATER LEVEL WARNING: This section of the river is best fished during lower water periods. Any rise above normal water levels makes this stretch inaccessible and can become dangerous.

FISHING EXPERIENCE: Weirs Rapids is an excellent place for kayakers to blaze through some exciting rapids. It is also the last larger section of rapids before moving upstream to Providence Dam. The farther fishermen push upstream the slower the fishing becomes. At Weirs Rapids there are a few large holes and several sections of rapids which are ideal fishing locations for walleye.

      Primarily male walleyes will venture this far upstream. Early in the year fish have not swam this far upstream but late in the season this becomes more productive. Additionally there are a number of resident walleye that live in the deeper water between Weirs Rapids and Memorial Park. Often during the post spawn periods this is a more productive area. The rapids are strong and the holes are very deep, use caution when fishing these rapids. Walleye can be caught all the way up to Providence Dam in Grand Rapids but relatively few walleye swim that far upstream.

Boat Launch

FARNSWORTH PARK
A very nice cement boat launch is available at Farnsworth Metropark 8505 S. River Road (US 24), Waterville Ohio. This is available to the public providing opportunities for some fishing year-round.

475 BRIDGE BOAT LAUNCH
Under the 475 bridge in on River Road is a public access Side Cut Metropark for shallow boats. This is a single boat access point, gravel bottom with no dock available.

ORLEANS PARK BOAT LAUNCH
In Perrysburg Ohio there is a shallow boat launch that is available to the public. This is located at 655 Maumee Western Reserve Perrysburg Ohio. There is no dock available and during the run many fishermen are wader fishing around this access point.

MAPLE STREET BOAT LAUNCH
Farther downstream the Maple Street Launch is located off East Front Street at Maple Street in Perrysburg Ohio there is a deeper water boat launch with a dock. This is available to the public.

SCHROEDER FARM CAMPGROUND
In the heart of the prime walleye habitat is a privately owned boat launch that is open during walleye season. This is located at 27841 W River Rd, Perrysburg, Ohio. This is privately owned, access is available for a fee.

COREY STREET BOAT LAUNCH
The Corey Street Launch is located in at the end of Corey Street in Maumee Ohio farther downstream from the rapids. This is a city maintained small-boat launch ramp.

Chapter 15

Angler Respect

It might seem insane to stand three feet away from another angler. But that is exactly how crowded it gets during the peak of the Maumee Walleye Run. If everyone continues to cast directly in front of themselves, line tangles are minimal. Everyone is out to have fun and enjoy this magnificent outdoor sport. Fishing is about enjoying yourself, the outdoors, and the great resources Ohio provides. It is not worth getting frustrated and angry; no fish is worth that type of aggravation. With that being said, each year I have the pleasure of reuniting with old friends and meeting many new people. It's a time of year I look forward to and enjoy the many different people that partake in the sport.

Any time you pack thousands of people into close quarters the most important aspect becomes the respect that each person represents. While standing shoulder to shoulder you will meet many interesting people. For me it is a place where the playing field is level. Whether you are a Vice President of a large corporation, a steel worker, or receptionist; we're all equally chasing after the same fish. It is this spring run of walleye which pulls so many of us together from all walks of life. These friendships keep me coming back year after year.

These two fishermen are working together to net a nice walleye.

But let's talk about how to make fishing a memorable experience for everyone down the river banks. New anglers partaking in the spring walleye run are often amazed at how close together anglers are standing. Sometimes it seems like people are almost touching shoulders. Ideally this is not the best situation. Between each person you need five plus feet. This gives you the space to handle fish and room to breathe. While I am fishing next to my brother I can literally stand on his toes but we have been fishing the river together our entire lives. We fish in a similar fashion and know when to get out of the way. Unless you have a similar brotherly connections do not walk in and fish that close to a stranger. They will not appreciate the gesture.

Several years back a friend of mine, Mike, called me up late in the evening during mid-April asking me to take him fishing. My answer was simple, "Meet me at 5:00 a.m. and I'll get you into some hot fishing action." Mike showed up but since he didn't have much time to prepare and wanted to borrow some equipment. I only had one small tackle box of lures which was plenty to share for the morning.

Each time Mike wanted to borrow another lure he reached

When everyone works together and casts directly in front of themselves even on busy days anglers can stay tangle free.

into my fishing jacket to pull out the tackle box of lures. All morning Mike stood next to me losing more and more lures. Finally during the late morning Mike was reaching for another lure while I was casting. I quickly snapped my rod back and my hook swung around, grazed his cheek, and hooked his hat. Off it went flying out into the river. Lucky for Mike my hook was still in his hat which was quickly recovered. That was the catch of the day. Interesting enough Mike never borrowed another lure for the rest of the day. Hat's off to you Mike!

I was lucky, that incident could have ended with a trip to the emergency room. I should have been more aware of his presence. With so many walleye being caught, tangled lines and hands in the water you need to watch what you are doing. There are times when fishing line is tangled up with someone downstream and another fisherman picks up those lures from the water. Be aware of the situation and do not yank or pull. A hook in the hand is not a pleasant experience. Make sure you are setting the hook on a walleye not your neighbor fisherman. For many, walleye are hard to come by, so when fishing near others please make sure to stay in line with the other fishermen. Walking out in front of others will cause you to get a hook in the leg of your waders and bump fish off other fisherman's lines that are upstream.

Fishing is an exciting sport. Although the Maumee River boasts to have exceptional walleye fishing there are many times it takes several hours to finally get a bite. The rush of adrenalin pulses through my veins as I work the fish into my net. Along the way there are so many obstacles to overcome while the toothy walleye fights back. With any opportunity they are willing to throw your hook. To eliminate one of the many obstacles of landing a walleye, stay clear when others are fighting a fish. So many times walleye get tangled into another fisherman's line or waders, step back and let them land the fish. Walleye have a mind of their own; do your best to stay clear.

Paying attention to where, when and how you cast will avoid many tangles. Time your cast so you are casting at the same time or after those anglers nearby, this will avoid hanging up on them. Getting into a good rhythm with those around you will make for an enjoyable outing. Work hard to avoid casting over other fishermen's lines that are upstream; this will inevitably cause lines to get tangled up. The best advice is to cast straight out in front, at 12 or 1 o'clock. Watch how others are fishing nearby. Are they casting longer or shorter? Additionally, letting your lure hang too long straight downstream in the water while others immediately real in their lures will cause a tangle. Watch those around you for the style and adapt if necessary. Timing is everything when casting.

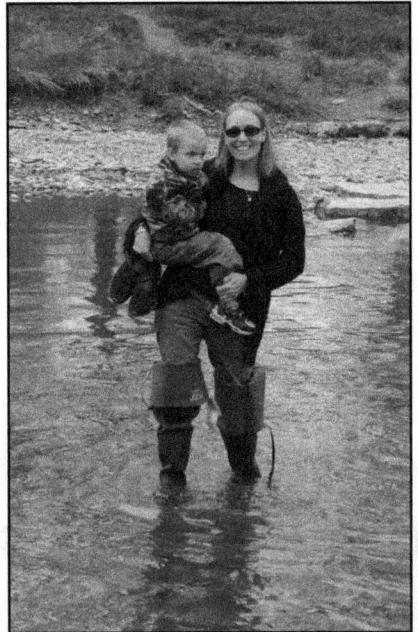

Thousands of people rush to the banks for a short six weeks during the walleye run. Be mindful that we share the river with many others who enjoy the Maumee River; children, bird watchers, local neighborhoods, and many others. Respect the resources available to us.

Tangles and tying lures are part of fishing the river. Pre-tying floating jig head leaders is a way to speed up the process.

Anytime there are fishermen crammed along the back a few lines will get tangled. This type of fishing pressure is a part of the Maumee River. It's ok to cut the jig off if the lures and lines are tangled into a spider web. It's best to cut your own rig off if possible, whether the tangle was your fault or not. Giving this amount of headway will go a long way. After a tying on a few thousand jigs I have become rather quick at tying and retying. Instead of working to untangle a mess for several minutes I would rather take 30 seconds to re-tie. It is best to not hold onto snags forever, just cut and tie. But never cut someone's fishing lines in the middle of their line. Fishing line is expensive, especially the popular braided line. Doing this is a sure way to ignite a furious conversation along with frustration.

While in the river fishing my rule is to "ask first." Some fishermen appreciate a helping hand while others are very private. With so many people smashed into one small location you have a wide variety of personalities. Even if you think you are being helpful by landing their fish, ask first. For me, I'm confident in my fish handling skills and would rather land all my own fish. I've seen too many people loose fish in their hands because of mishandling. And if I lose my own fish, it's my fault. I have no one to blame but myself. So if you're lending a hand make sure to ask before proceeding.

Maumee River walleye fishing is primarily known for fisherman stacked shoulder to shoulder along the banks. Another way to tackle the river is by launching small boats at one of the many ramps. As boaters the river is wide and long with walleye filling the waters from Maumee Bay all the way to the first dam. With such a wide array of spots to select from it is a wonder why boaters find their way within casting distance of shoreline fisherman. Unfortunately I have seen boats clobbered with lead weights and hooks casted over the bow because the boaters anchored too close to the

shore. This type of activity is nonsense and disrespectful. With the crowds growing, stacking the shores with fishermen looking for a walleye meal the boats should search out those secluded holes in the mainstream. If the area they want to fish is within casting distance of shoreline fishermen they should strap on a pair of waders and come on shore.

Not all the land along the Maumee River is public ground. We have been blessed with Side Cut Metropark that stretches through a large section of the spawning ground. We need to respect the private land. This does not mean we cannot fish the river in front of those areas we simply need to access it from the water.

In the same token the massive walleye spawn brings thousands of anglers to the banks. Let's continue to do our part keeping the land and water pristine. Pull out any broken and leftover line while in the water. We need to do our part by keeping the ground clean and picking up litter along the way.

In my years on the water I've seen just about everything on the water. I've had so many great days and met up with many kind people on the water. There are many friends I only see during spring walleye run and at the yearend we disband to our home towns. It's a huge community that comes together during this one time of year. Those are the times that I remember the most, the friendships and those who I will see in the upcoming year.

Chapter 16

Ohio Department of Natural Resources

Standing in the river waiting for the sun to rise I reached down to scoop up a handful of water. It was so cold I could feel it down into my bones as I let the water trickle through my fingers back into the river. Listening to the splashing sound, I slowly raised my head to gaze across the pristine, gently rippled surface of the river.

The honking of geese broke the morning silence; each honk was crisp and clear. Emerging from the fog overhead were a dozen geese organized in a V shape and following the river upstream. In a moment they disappeared and the honks faded away. It was almost time for the first cast. The earliest rays of the morning sun crested the horizon sending a beautiful shaft of light upward to the heavens.

Across the river, a dark figure appeared from the fog. I quickly recognized the dark shape walking toward the river to be an Ohio Department of Natural Resources (ODNR) Wildlife Officer. He placed a tripod with a spotting scope mounted to the top in plain sight directly across from me. With only two other fishermen in that stretch of the river, I was under the microscope. The scene was like an old western standoff; we were face to face while I fished and he closely watched my every move.

On that particular day the ODNR Wildlife Officer was very

bold, making his presence known. Most often, surveillance is done under the cover of the trees, hidden from nearby fisherman. Either way, being observed is a frequent part of fishing on the Maumee River. The ODNR is very active about surveying the fishermen. This group of dedicated individuals works hard to protect the species to ensure the walleye run continues far into the future.

WALLEYE WARS

In the 1980's and prior, snagging walleye was common practice, with fishermen using oversized and bent hooks, and placing fish on stringers below the water. Was it right? No. But it was very common for a fisherman to snag walleye or have the person next to him snag a fish. Today the situation is very different.

Since 2000 there has been a great movement away from this problem, with several factors leading to this shift. Paul Kurfis, law enforcement supervisor for Wildlife District Two, indicates, "The floating jig head really helped change that problem." This new technique makes it easier to catch fish while making it harder to snag a fish. Additionally, the ODNR worked hard to step up enforcement while educating the public. Lastly, the fisherman's perception changed drastically. A cultural conflict arose between fishermen from earlier generations and those with today's conservationist viewpoint. Someone who is not law abiding during the walleye run is not tolerated by many of today's river walleye fishermen. Today, many fishermen accept the challenge to catch a legal walleye, and they enjoy the sport more than ever.

Following are the most common violations they cite during the Maumee River Walleye Run.
- Fishing without a license
- Overbag walleye
- Fail to release/possess snagged walleye
- Hook violation
- Fish before/after hours
- Undersize walleye
- Stream Litter

Historically the violations for "possess snagged walleye" were much greater. In the more recent years, there have been great strides to enforce the rules Floating jig heads have become the pre-

This snagged walleye was quickly released back for another day.

dominant equipment, and these jigs have a harder time snagging a fish. Also, many of the prior years had much higher creel limits, making taking "over the limit" of walleye uncommon. In recent years creel limits have been reduced greatly. These two changes have had opposite effects. While snagged walleye violations have drastically decreased, "overbag" violations have steadily increased.

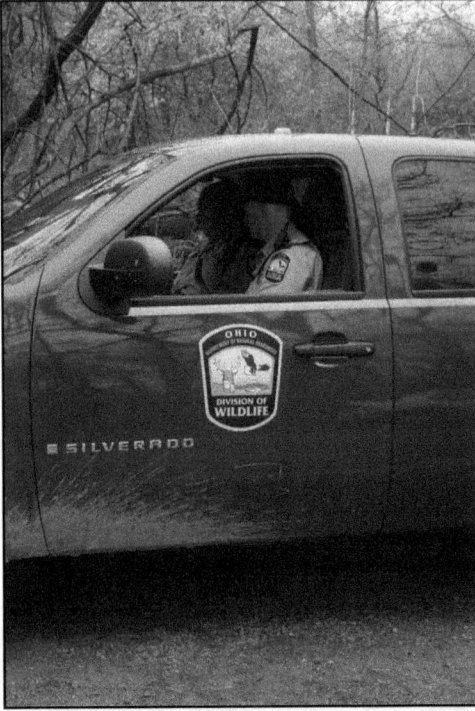

ODNR Wildlife Officers work hard to enforce the rules along the Maumee River. It takes a tremendous amount of surveillance and those in violation of the regulations are cited with tickets.

With so many walleye concentrated in one small location, it is tempting for fishermen to become overzealous and violate the rules. So how does the ODNR enforce the walleye run? Kurfis indicated there is a lot of surveillance done along the river during the run. Wildlife Officers from across the entire state report to the banks to help with the effort. On any given day there are from four to twenty Wildlife Officers working the river banks. It is not uncommon to see officers spotting fishermen from vehicles or set up along the banks. In addition to surveillance, the ODNR Officers are making their presence known by checking for valid fishing licenses and walking the shorelines and park entrances.

What the ODNR does to enforce the rules takes surveillance to the next level. These Wildlife Officers are set up much like deer hunters awaiting their prey. The officers dress in camouflage, setting themselves up in brush piles. With high-powered spotting scopes, they can watch fishermen at long ranges, including across the river. So even though they may not be standing next to you, spotting scopes allow officers to be there visually when they are actually

Side Cut Metropark Rangers care for the people using the park. They do their best to inform the anglers of the regulations while protecting people from unseen dangers.

positioned across the river. Communication with other Wildlife Officers also allows them to be in contact with other Wildlife Officers that cite game violators. Additionally, extensive documentation, including video and photography, is used to monitor those attempting to make a second trip to take home an extra daily creel limit.

So far, I have only discussed the most visible Wildlife Officers patrolling on foot; I have not even discussed those Wildlife Officer in plain clothes placed in problem areas of the river. So the guy fishing next to you or watching from shore could be a Wildlife Officer getting a closer look at the situation. Learning about all the different layers of surveillance was surreal; I realized that the spring run draws as much attention from Wildlife Officers as it does from fishermen.

Along with the Wildlife Officers patrolling on foot, using spotting scopes, and blending with the crowd in plain clothes, ODNR has also enlisted the help of the fishermen themselves. In 1982 the ODNR implemented the "Turn In a Poacher (TIP)" program. This program began involving the public to help report wildlife crimes. This has been a big aid to the Wildlife Officers, as they are receiving information while offenses are actually occurring. Upon receiving tips, Wildlife Officers immediately report to the area for further investigation of the reports. The TIP line is 1-800-POACHER.

Danger-Hazardous Water Levels

DO NOT CROSS TO THE ISLAND

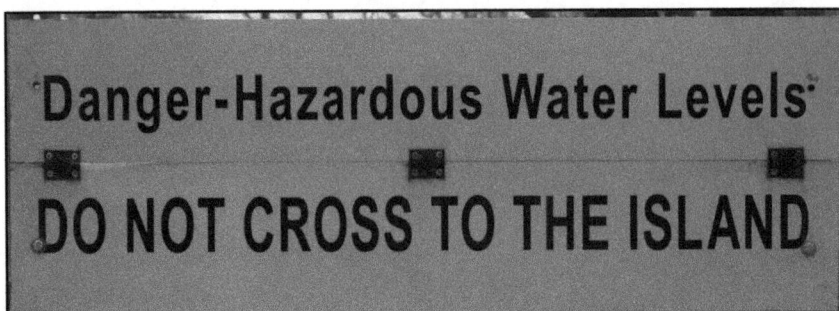

To protect those using the Metropark, crossing to Blue Grass Island is closed when the water rises above 582 feet above sea level.

METROPARK INVOLVEMENT

The scurry of the spring run can bring disruptions to the cities of Maumee and Perrysburg, with the rush of fishermen in the area causing disruption. Fortunately, there are many organizations that have worked together to make the fisheries enjoyable for all who partake. The Side Cut Metropark goes out of its way to greet everyone visiting with open arms. They have developed programs and recycling specifically designed for the spring audience.

Park rangers take pride in the fishery and therefore become knowledgeable of the fishing regulations. Although they work closely with the ODNR, Metropark Rangers let the Wildlife Officers handle the game violations. Caring for the park resources and visitors becomes the primary concern of the rangers. This entails maintenance to ensure the Metropark is clean and beautiful, managing traffic, educating those visitors about the resources, and keeping all visitors safe.

One of the most fished islands in the Side Cut Metropark is Blue Grass Island. Once the water levels rise 582 feet above sea level, crossing to the island becomes unsafe. The normal river level is typically 580 feet above sea level. To improve awareness they have implemented signs along the river to indicate if you can or cannot cross. Crossing once the signs are posted is a Metropark violation. While fishing, it can be hard to tell how much the water level has increased, so this is a way for the Metropark rangers to keep everyone safe from harm. Scott Carpenter, Public Relations Director at Metroparks of the Toledo Area indicated, "If a fisherman is rescued the

Cross to Bluegrass Island At Your Own Risk

Crossing to Blue Grass Island can be difficult for a novice when the water level just dips just below 582 feet above sea level. The channel has big rocks and several deep holes.

Maumee Fire Department can bill them for the services provided."

After the walleye run is over, there is tremendous clean-up necessary to enhance the area. There is a great amount of spent fishing line that can be a hazard to the birds. To help, the parks have set up designated fishing line recycle stations. The recycled line is then sent to an organization that uses it to create plastic fish habitat. This is a wonderful way for fishermen to give back to the environment after enjoying the use of the area's natural resources..

CONSERVING THE WALLEYE FISHERY

When I thought about the Department of Natural Resources ten years ago, my mind always focused on the conservation officers. These are the officers on the ground and are the face of the ODNR for many. After writing about the outdoor world for over ten years I have become aware of the people behind the scenes. Although we actually encounter the conservation officers, a much larger portion of the Department of Natural Resources are Biologists, Scientists, Public Relation specialists and many more.

The great fishing we have in the river has a direct correlation with the daily work done by the ODNR biologists. These individuals are working every day to understand the overall health of the walleye population and how we can continue to allow them to thrive. Each year there is a creel survey and fish assessment. Additionally, biologists are tracking how walleye move through the Great Lakes using a tagging program.

The creel survey assesses the fisherman's effort, success rates, and harvest sizes. This is a big project to assess angler success from all the marinas, wading and shoreline fishermen including the walleye run. Each year I have seen field biologists recording data during the peak season.

This is a tagged walleye ready to be returned to the water. If you ever catch a tagged walleye call the information into the ODNR.

The fish assessment gathers a massive amount of data for the ODNR, providing information about forage, fish populations, and health. There have been several large invasive species and chemicals that have had sizeable effects on Lake Erie. The invasive zebra mussel was one of the non-native species that seriously threatened the ecology of our lakes and streams. Another current concern is the elevated phosphorus levels. Much of the phosphorus level imbalance has been caused by man-made sources. With the continuing urbanization in the watershed of the Maumee River, ODNR biologists are working to help resolve these issues. The phosphorus level imbalance is widespread, but fortunately Lake Erie has shown us that it can recover quickly.

How many walleye fishermen have ever caught a walleye with a metal tag in his jaw bone? If you have, it is likely you are a regular Lake Erie fisherman. I have been lucky enough to catch one myself. Tags rely on fishermen catching the fish and then calling in the information, but the ODNR only gets 4% returned annually. These tags are used to help understand the movement, health, and growth of walleye. The walleye telemetry project has moved the ODNR forward in understanding both large and small scale walleye movement. They also have radio-tags placed on walleye within the Great Lakes and their tributaries. Additionally, many hydrophones are placed within the Great Lakes to take readings and ultimately understand how walleye move throughout the Great Lakes.

Ohio Department of Natural Resources

This walleye has been tagged for the walleye telemetry project. If one of these fish is caught notifying the ODNR will greatly help the ODNR biologists ensure we have a healthy future of fishing.

All of the information gathered from this research has helped protect the annual walleye run. Everything the biologists handle, from improving the spawning habitat, taking important steps to improve the water quality, and even managing creel limits, helps ensure there will continue to be a robust spring run far into the future. When thinking about the Department of Natural Resources, I appreciate the effort of the many individuals working to conserve our valuable fisheries.

Chapter 17

Safety on the Water

Did you know boats less than twenty-one feet long are the most common boats reported in accidents? Ninety percent of all victims who drown were not wearing a life jacket. One half of recreational boating fatalities happen in calm water. Many people drown close to shore but were not wearing a life jacket. Do you realize that most of the fishermen on the Maumee River do not wear a life jacket? Surviving an accident starts before you even head to the water with selecting the right equipment and properly wearing it on the water.

The water in the spring can run high and out of control. The turbulent water rushing downstream can sweep a fisherman into an unsafe part of the river very quickly. Even those safely fishing on Blue Grass Island can get trapped by quickly rising water.

Consider this: the water temperature is in the 30's towards the beginning of the season. Submerged in water this cold, your body muscles contract, joints become hard to move, and your body goes into shock! Now you are not thinking clearly and panic washes over you. You begin to thrash around. With a loss of bearings, this causes panic, and with the cold water being sucked into your lungs you could go into instant cardiac arrest. All of that happens in the first minute. Now it's time to survive! In 32 degree water you have less than 15 minutes before becoming exhausted and death occurs.

I am not telling this story to scare you; I am trying to awaken you to the sobering facts. Accidents happen every year. We head out for an enjoyable day on the water and it quickly turns into a tragedy. Several times a year I see a fisherman stumble over rocks and fall into the water. Just a few years ago I saw a fisherman go underwater, taking a ride down stream. Everyone scrambled when he did not come right back up. Those fifteen seconds were the longest moments of his life. His face was white when we pulled him to shore.

A few years later I saw a boater anchor his boat line from the stern during a higher water period. Water started rushing over the back of the boat with amazing speed. In a few seconds, the boat was full of water. The boaters had grabbed life jackets with only moments to spare. I could not believe this happened right in front of me. Standing along the shoreline in waders, there was nothing I could do to help. I have seen these accidents firsthand too many times. Once you see something of this gravity on the river you will take caution. You must be prepared when you are on the water; these precautionary steps could save your life.

WADER SAFETY

Much of the Maumee River Walleye Run is fished from waders on the shorelines. Waders are commonly used whether the water is raging high or low waters prevail. To be prepared, there are several recommended lifesaving items, including life jackets, wader belts, and wading sticks. A list of life jackets has already been covered in the equipment checklist. Life jackets are not just for boaters; those wading the river should also use them. I used to hate my life jacket and went for years without wearing it. I have since found an inflatable version that is very comfortable. This made the difference, and now I wear it often.

In water, waders are weightless. Wader belts are a safety device designed to keep water out of the wader legs. All too often I see fishermen without wader belts strapped on to hold out the water. Wader sticks are another valuable piece of safety equipment. Today there are collapsible walking sticks that help navigate heavy current and aid in locating rocks. Submerged rocks are what catch people by surprise most often. When walking, shuffle your feet along the

At the end of the day no fish is more important then returning home to your family.

bottom. This will help you find the rocks before they find you.

Every year I see several fishermen fall into the river because they either lose their balance or walk into an unseen rock. One of my friends, Tim, was quickly walking from one fishing location to another and hit one of those unseen rocks. He went completely under the water before he was able to regain his footing. After this embarrassing event Tim just stood up, took off his wet clothes, and continued fishing. Unfortunately it was a cold windy morning, not an easy day to air dry. And to top it off, he took home a limit of fish. Now that is dedication.

This time the situation ended up okay, but not all of them finish like this one. I want everyone to think about the situation before it happens. What happens if you fall into the water? In a calm area, stand up and regain your composure. Fortunately, this is what happened to Tim. If you get swept downstream, ride the current until you can reach secure ground. If you are swept into dangerous water, get rid of your gear and swim aggressively, angling towards calmer water. Swimming with waders is not easy but it is possible. Do not stand until you reach a calm spot.

I grew up on the river, so navigating the impressive rapids comes naturally. Every year I bring a few new people out to experience the excitement of river fishing. One of my dear friends loves walleye fishing, but she is not too excited about the current so we use the buddy system. This is a good method to apply when targeting the rapids with someone who is unsure of their ability. You secure the person and break the current for them. Walk on the upstream side, breaking the current for them. Both fishermen should hold the other person's wader straps. That way, if their hands slip, you've got them. And they can brace on you if their footing has a problem. Then when they're setting their feet, you keep holding onto their wader straps until they are sure they are stable and ready. I often find myself fishing upstream in order to break the current the entire time. This is the easiest way for two people with different experience levels to cross heavy current.

The force of the water can be great, but the way you stand can make resisting it much easier. Keep a stance as wide as your shoulders to provide a stable foundation for your body. If you allow the water to push sideways around your legs, it has one third less force than when you face the current. When the current is pushing against both legs and possibly the lower body, the most force will be presented. This can cause a loss of balance. After fishing for hours in the spring water, legs become cold and stiff. One wrong move could be dangerous. A walking stick really helps improve footing when walking or turning around in heavy current. Plant the walking stick into the ground before lifting your leg to turn around.

Survival Time with Different Water Temperatures

Water Temperature	Exhaustion	Death
32.5	Under 15 min.	15 min. or less
32.5-40	15-30 min.	30-90 min.
40-50	30-60 min.	1-3 hrs.
50-60	30-60 min.	1-6 hrs.
60-70	2-7 hrs.	2-40 hrs.
70-80	3-12 hrs.	3 hrs.-indefinite

*Provided by ODNR Division of Watercraft

Small boats provide access to great walleye structure on the Maumee River but always be prepared with the appropriate lifejackets.

BOAT SAFETY

Boat safety is not to be taken lightly. Small boats swarm into the river when high waters limit the fishing to fewer shoreline locations. This is a good time to navigate without running into rocks, but there are far more dangers present during higher water than during lower water. To do safety justice, it is time to get serious about navigating the "mighty Maumee" with a small craft boat.

Many of the boats fishing the river range from 12 to 16 foot and have smaller engines. The ODNR Division of Watercraft considers these small craft boats. While very useful during these high water periods, these are small vessels and require caution when being operated during high water. Things can go wrong with a small boat on a rushing river. For most of the walleye run the water temperature is hovering around 40 degrees Fahrenheit. Water that cold will put a person into shock very quickly.

The river is unforgiving; higher water drastically increases the flow rate, making small engines not powerful enough to navigate the hazardous waters. All too often, I watch small boats fly downstream then barely make it back upstream to the boat ramp.

Brian Miller and Jeff Miller are all smiles after returning safely from a successful day on the river.

Some of them are moving slower than those walking the shoreline; this is an unsettling experience. At that rate the driver has little control. Match your horsepower to the currents and do not under power your boat.

Wearing life jackets at all times is recommended by the ODNR Division of Watercraft. ODNR Division of Watercraft also stated that it is important for life jackets to be worn when the boater cannot swim, when the boater is boating alone, when the water is dangerously cold, in rough water, during severe weather, and in a fast current. These water conditions all nicely describe the Maumee River.

The majority of boating accidents are preventable. Poor decisions and mistakes cause boaters to get into dangerous situations. But accidents do happen, so here are some tips to remember if you happen to have trouble on the river. If you fall overboard, get back in. If your boat has capsized, climb onto the boat to get as much of your body out of the cold water as possible. When in danger keep your wits about you and react appropriately. Keep your head above water, concentrate on breathing, and tread water until safety arrives.

However, being safe in the first place is far better than having to react to danger. Stay seated when under way. Put on a life jacket and wear it at all times. Inspect your life jacket before heading out. Small boats can only carry a few people, so know those limits. Know your boat; the river can be dangerous. Always secure the anchor line to the bow (front) of the boat, never to the stern (rear). The boat I saw take on water was anchored from the stern. It took seconds for water to rush over the back of the boat and cause an emergency situation.

The river is full of rocks and reefs that will tear up a prop. When water rises, many of the reefs and rocks are barely submerged. As if watching for rocks was not enough, floating debris is an even greater problem. High water brings down full trees that float downstream. A quick release anchor is the best way to deal with any large debris that may take you by surprise.

This is a brief list of the dangers and safety guidelines on the river. The Ohio Division of Watercraft has a tremendous amount of boating resources available for free that cover these topics in greater detail. Please review the Ohio Division of Watercraft information for boating education courses, the Ohio boat operator's guide, and the required safety equipment.

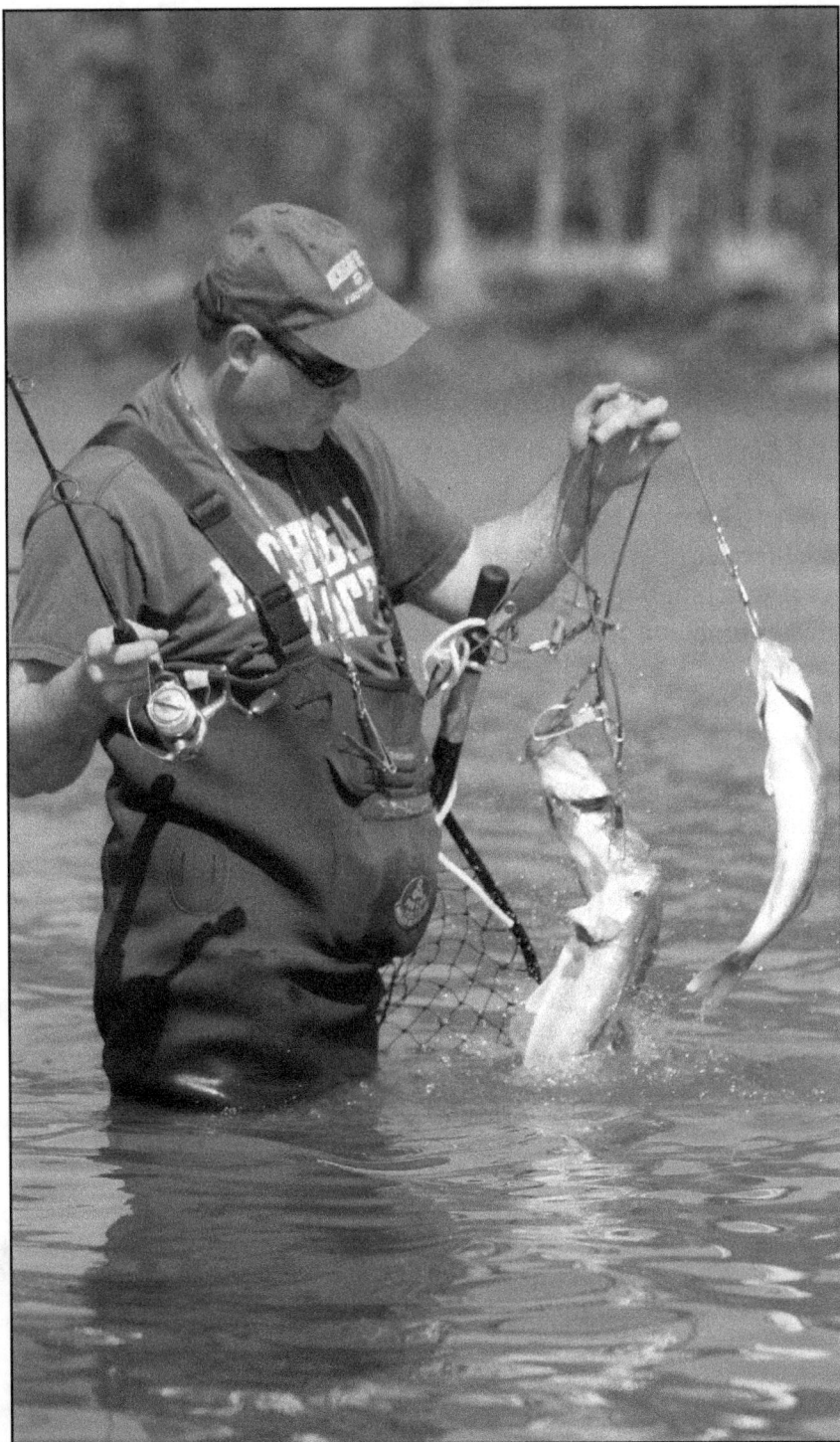

Chapter 18

Walleye Resources

In the fast pace world today of online mobile devices and tablets everywhere people want information faster than ever. I want to know the river height before deciding to go fishing. I also want to know where the fish are and if I am going to get my limit. All of this I want before leaving work in another state, miles away from the Maumee River.

The walleye run is a big deal. People from all walks of life come to enjoy the bountiful fishing. This is their vacation from the world. Taking in the walleye for what it is, spectacular. We are lucky today to have more resources available than ever before. There are multiple fishing reports, water level and temperature gauges, online communities, and many different forms of tackle distribution channels. All of these resources are beneficial to the river fisherman.

TACKLE SHOPS

The Maumee River is known for eating up jigs on the rocky bottom. Needless to say you will need to have a stockpile to get you through the season. There are a couple local shops that keep stock in the hottest colors and best floaters for the Maumee River. Some of these local tackle shops work with local fishermen to understand what colors are working best. Then they have create new color and color combinations that work in the river. These shops listen to the cus-

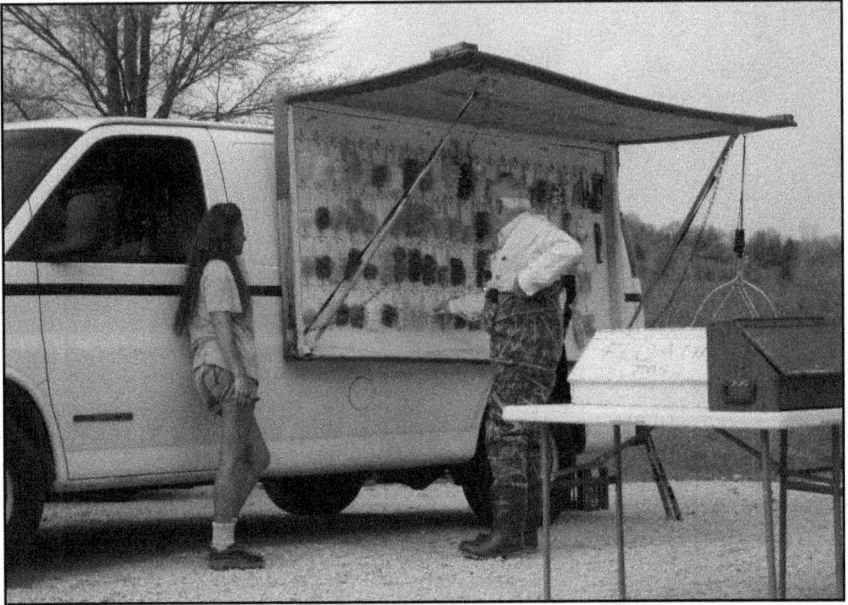

Roadside tackle dealers have a great selection of lures. There are several scattered along the shoreline.

tomers and make tackle designed specifically for the Maumee River. Aside from tackle their vicinity to the river is ideal if a fisherman is short on gear. Tackle shops also are talking to fishermen every day so they know every little detail about the river. If the fish are biting, the river rises, or a new run of walleye move in these shops are on the front line. Use their insight on the conditions and utilize what they have to offer.

PORTABLE TACKLE DEALERS

Arrived on location and forgot something important? Not a problem. Along the road are portable tackle dealers. These dealers move in, setup shop, and are a wealth of information. They have saved me a few times by carrying everything from jigs to reels. Just last year one of my reels started grinding really bad. I was there early so I could enjoy several hours on the water and now every turn of the handle was painful. Instead of packing it in these guys had a replacement so I could enjoy the rest of the afternoon.

There is more there then a tackle dealer. These guys are watching fisherman all day long. They see when the limits are being

Real time information from a reliable source can be the most deadly resource for being extremely successful on the Maumee River.

taken, hear what color works, know the height, and see where the fishing is hot. There is nobody else that spends as much time watching fish being caught then these dealers. Over the years I have relied on their information. I figure buying some tackle to swap for that information is priceless. The information that I have gathered has paid for itself many times over.

FISHING REPORTS

The heart and blood of river fishing is communicated through fishing reports. Several locations work to provide information; tackle shops, walleye hotline, and local bait dealers. Many different people come together to help pull off the reporting that hits the river each year. Much of this information includes water temperatures, water level, water clarity, angler success, and lure success.

One of the longest standing reports comes from Side Cut Metropark which provides a Walleye Hotline that is updated whenever conditions change. This information consists of water levels and temperature, and fishing success. (419) 407-9731.The Ohio Department of Natural Resources also provides river fishing reports that are wide scoping on the entire region therefore less helpful for day to day activity. Local tackle shops have provided the best daily information for fishermen. This often includes reports of the best lures and pictures from successful anglers.

Outside of those official reports are Facebook and online communities from the local businesses and tackle dealers. These make it easy for fishermen from afar to check in on the action before making the long drive in town.

ONLINE COMMUNITIES

Online Communities have been around for years, most recently there are several focused on the Maumee River. These communities' help these addicts bring the fishing to them at work or home. From

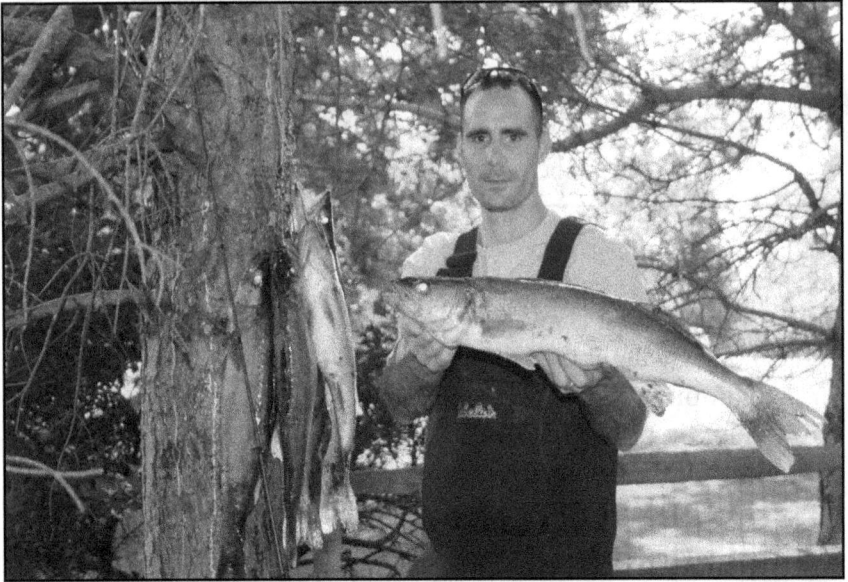

The spring walleye run is a traditional event that keeps me coming back every year. This is an amazing experience that I hope many others will enjoy far into the future.

these communities people can keep tabs on other successful fishermen. Watching and contributing help others find fishing locations and understand what others are doing to be successful. Techniques are improved upon each year, by learning from others experience it can shave years off an angler's learning curve.

BAND OF BROTHERS

There is nothing like on the spot reports coming from a trusted source. Over the years I have built a community of fishermen that I trust. If the fishing is on, I get a call. If someone is struggling, help is only a phone call away. These people have been fishing for years and I trust their every word. I encourage everyone to have a "Band of Brothers" they can rely on. Someone in this group is fishing every day of the run whether it's the pre-spawn or post-spawn. If I need to know if it is worth the drive then I can get that information. Create a community of your own by getting to know other local fishermen. This has helped me in all avenues of life whether it be fishing, hunting, or in the business world.

www.ingramcontent.com/pod-product-compliance
Lightning Source LLC
Chambersburg PA
CBHW062222270326
41930CB00009B/1828